THE
RETURN

THE RETURN

REFLECTIONS ON LOVING GOD BACK

LACEY STURM

BakerBooks

a division of Baker Publishing Group
Grand Rapids, Michigan

© 2018 by Lacey Sturm

Published by Baker Books
a division of Baker Publishing Group
PO Box 6287, Grand Rapids, MI 49516-6287
www.bakerbooks.com

Printed in the United States of America

Library of Congress Cataloging-in-Publication Data
Names: Sturm, Lacey, author.
Title: The return : reflections on loving God back / Lacey Sturm.
Description: Grand Rapids : Baker Publishing Group, 2018. | Includes
    bibliographical references and index.
Identifiers: LCCN 2017053751 | ISBN 9780801016752 (pbk. : alk. paper)
Subjects: LCSH: God (Christianity)—Worship and love. | Christian life.
Classification: LCC BV4817 .S76 2018 | DDC 248.4—dc23
LC record available at https://lccn.loc.gov/2017053751

Some names and details have been changed to protect the privacy of the individuals involved.

All illustrations by Joshua Sturm.

Published in association with Yates & Yates, www.yates2.com.

18 19 20 21 22 23 24   7 6 5 4 3 2 1

For Mom: You are a wild work of God's art. You are a powerful eternal poetic song from heaven. You are a constant reminder that I can access superhuman strength and perseverance when the whole world is telling me to give up. The song of your life gets stuck in my head so often and I know I can survive anything while it's playing. Love you. Sweet tights.
Lacey Nicole

For Joshua Lewis and Arrow David Sturm.
I pray that my ceiling would be your floor.
Burn brightly, Dad

CONTENTS

The rule of no realm is mine, neither of Gondor nor any other, great or small. But all worthy things that are in peril as the world now stands, those are my care. And for my part, I shall not wholly fail of my task, though Gondor should perish, if anything passes through this night that can still grow fair or bear fruit and flower again in days to come. For I also am a steward. Did you not know?

J. R. R. Tolkien, *The Return of the King*

DEAR READER

Every morning I thank God for another day. I've lived through seasons of facing death daily, in all kinds of ways. Surviving has taught me that each morning is a gift. In this thankful moment of waking up, I long to come close to God. I long to sit in his arms and hear him breathe, and in a childlike way, as I used to do in my mother's arms, try to get my breath to line up with his. This is when I ask God questions. I know that the answers are somewhere in his breath. The Bible says all Scripture is God-breathed.

So I ask God questions in the morning while we sit together, and I listen to his answers in the Scriptures. Then I begin to journal, and revelation comes. What you hold in your hands now are pieces of my journals.

At night I curl back up in his arms and listen. With the Scriptures, it's like God is singing us all this eternal song, with movements of emotion, history, adventure, passion, joy, suffering, justice, mercy, and mystery. I love to end my day with his thoughts as well, reading through the Bible as a story. While I read and after, I talk to God, thanking him and praying for understanding, transformation, help, wisdom, and all kinds of things.

In response to his song over me, I want to sing to him in return. Writing poems and songs helps me to bring him my heart.

God's love is poured into my soul during our times together. This makes me want to love others. So I make plans to love and serve. Some ways I like to serve are to cook, clean, and give my favorite books away. You will find this pattern in my journal.

I read the Scriptures in the morning and in the evening.

I pray. I just talk to God and write him letters.

I write poems and new song ideas—many times this turns into music.

I write recipes with love and joy. I like to love by being artistic with organization, encouragement, and food.

To-do lists help put Random Acts of Kindness (or RAKs) into my day on purpose. I also make plans to steward my health with exercise, my mind with books, my relationships with giving, and my opportunities by making the most of them. I write these out in my to-do lists as well.

Finally, I journal. Loving God back in all these ways has caused my soul to grow.

I am returning my gifts.

Without God's direction to know his purpose for the gifts he gives, I often make a mess of them. When I bring my gifts back to him, he is excited for me to discover the potential for glory he has hidden in each one.

Life is filled with opportunities to glorify God with our choices. When I make a choice about what to do with relationships, time, work, or resources, this choice is a way to manage the goodness, that thing I'm called to do.

In my journals, I seek answers to questions like How do I sense what I'm supposed to do? How do I know what I'm called to?

What does it look like to live a life of responding to the love of God by *loving him back?*

This will look different for each of us. There are unique challenges for each of us in every season and unique victories for us to claim.

My journey looks like a winding road, with ups and downs, construction zones, and vistas. It began with me playing guitar at a club meeting in high school and has meandered on to many surprises, like becoming a rock star, a wife, a mom, a writer, a speaker, and now a solo artist with a sporadically touring family.

Each season holds its own special significance.

I hope what I reflect on here inspires you to bravely say yes to God. These flashes of my journals will let you see how the key to living my greatest adventure is following the Spirit as I travel this winding road.

For ten years, my husband, Josh, and I have journeyed together. He has this magical gift of expressing ideas through images and art. His voice is key in fully expressing to you our adventures in following the Spirit.

The Bible says we don't know where the wind goes—it's unpredictable. That's what it's like to follow God. When we follow God's Spirit, it makes us free and keeps us there. It forces us to break out of cages the world builds, to disintegrate our judgments, and to follow his true way of freedom.

The Return is a diary of my Spirit Wind Travels.

Following him.

Growing in his love.

And doing my best to live like the wind, returning God's love and life by honoring the gifts he's given me.

INTRODUCTION

BECOME A ROCK STAR?

As I stood signing autographs at the club, the line stretched out the door. A sixteen-year-old girl and her mom walked over to me.

Both mother and daughter had petite frames and lovely, wild manes of dark black curls. The sixteen-year-old started talking quickly, her braces sparkling.

"Oh my gosh, I can't believe I'm actually meeting you. I have been your fan for such a long time; I love all your songs, and your albums are my favorite ever. They mean so much to me and you have helped me through so much and I just wanted to ask you so many things—and oh my gosh, I'm so sorry, I don't want to take up too much of your time, there are so many people here."

Her mom put her hand on her shoulder and spoke up, a little embarrassed. "Just tell her what you want to tell her; there are people waiting."

She rolled her eyes and forcefully shrugged her mom's hand off as if to say, "Don't touch me!"

I saw the hurt in her mother's face and felt it like an arrow to my own heart as a mother. The daughter went quickly from embarrassment to anger to sadness and turned away.

I glanced down to see the deep scars on the inside of her arms that ran all the way down to her wrists. She was nervously fidgeting with the fringe on her black-and-white striped fingerless gloves. I recognized her. I had seen her picture over and over. She was a fan who always commented on our social media. I had looked her up a few times because I found her delightfully artistic and witty. She also had posted a cover of our song "Run to You," playing guitar and singing along. Getting to meet her in person felt like a gift from God.

I reached up and grabbed her hands. "Anna!"

She turned back to look at me in disbelief. She gasped, "How do you know my name?"

"I recognize you from your posts. You have a great voice!"

"Wow!" She just stared at me.

I smiled back, so thankful for her, so full of the love of God for her. What a gift it is to feel God's love for a stranger, so deeply and completely—there is nothing like it.

Looking down at her feet, she said, "There is something I did want to ask you." She looked behind her, worrying about the line. I grabbed her hand again, smiled, and saw no one else at all.

"Yes?"

Blushing, she inhaled deeply and held her breath. She lifted her face to the lights, like they would give her language for this magical moment. "So how do you . . . I mean . . . what did you do . . . like, if I wanted to. I mean, what did you do, or how did you . . . I'm sorry. I don't know what I'm trying to say."

She looked down at her feet again, fidgeting with her gloves, undoubtedly hearing inner voices that were calling her stupid. I hated those voices. I knew how brilliant and lovely she was.

My heart was overflowing with love for her. I could see God had hidden so much within her—gifts for her to bless the world around her.

"How did I become a rock star, and how can you do something like what I do?" I offered, trying to help.

"Yes!" She breathed out all the air she had been holding in and relaxed with a giggle, as if to say thank you. This was such a common question from fans.

But the answer was so much more than I could share in a five-minute meet and greet. The first thing I wanted to do was hug her soul and tell her, "You are beautiful." I wanted her to know that God had amazing things in mind for her openhanded yesses to him. I wanted her to know that she was strong and brave. She had everything she needed for the adventure God wanted to lead her on.

I wanted to tell her why I wouldn't wish fame on my worst enemy and at the same time how important it was for her to let the Lord use her life for great glory.

I wanted her to know that her time was precious and that there were seasons for things. I wanted her to know that music comes from somewhere much deeper than just making art for art's sake.

I wanted her to know that her uniqueness was the most important thing. Though she could learn and grow from others, it was important that she was always becoming her truest self and not trying to be someone else.

I wanted her to know that her body was a gift and she should cherish it, not despise or abuse it.

I wanted her to know that her spirit and soul were even more important. She should nourish her heart more than anything else.

I wanted her to know how to honor herself. Her heart and soul, her relationships, her gifts and opportunities were presents from God to bring his glory to the world around her. I wanted her to know that her life would have a ripple effect that would impact everything around her.

I wanted her to know that she didn't have to settle for less than the heights of what God had called her to.

I wanted her to know that she could steward her life well. This is the greatest adventure. In the end, it is worth every bit of the pain, perseverance, and death it takes to live it.

But I couldn't say all these things in five minutes.

So I said, "God says that if we are faithful with a little, then we can be trusted with more.[1] We have to look at what is right in front of us, then figure out how to be faithful with it. When I was young, I hated myself and wanted to die. Then God rescued me and showed me that he could make me new if I would let him.

"So I opened my hands and said, 'I have no plans. What can you do with this life? Here I am, God, all yours.' If you will honestly hand everything over to him—your gifts, talents, relationships, your heart, your life . . . then he will give you so much more than you could ever dream up on your own."

I hugged her so tight, holding her as long as my tour manager would let me before he called the next person in line over. I hoped with all my heart that Anna would know how important she was. God loved her. He had great plans for her, if only she would trust him with her life. I prayed she would do well with all he had given her.

I moved on to the next person. The love overflowed once more.

There is no end to God's love for each of us. He loves us uniquely, because we have each been created uniquely.

No DNA like yours.

No perspective like yours.

No gifts just like yours.

Your purpose is important to all those around you.

I want you to see that there are so many gifts. They are available to enjoy, celebrate, and grow in. They are given from God to us to change the world for the better. I could never have imagined, in my wildest dreams, the life that God had in mind for me since I was conceived.

I believe God has dreams beyond our imagination for each one of us. I want to share some of my journey of stewarding life with

1. Matthew 25:23.

you. Perhaps it will help you step into the dream God has for you. He has hidden this abundant life like Easter eggs. We can run with joy, excitement, and expectation after it. We can lay down our lives for love and find true life in the process. We can give up our dreams and embrace God's dream. It has been hidden away in our hearts all along. It is so much more beautiful than any dream he may invite us to let die.

What will it be like when we face our Creator in eternity and he asks what we have earned with the talents he gave us? What *return* will we have gained for the one who invested everything? My hope is that we will make the most of every opportunity. This way we can rejoice that he is such a good Father to let us work alongside him—to be light like he is, loving and healing and bringing his peace, hope, and joy. Bringing the fullness of life that will redeem the dying world around us. Apart from him we can do nothing, but with God all things are possible.

> For we are co-workers in God's service; you are God's field, God's building. By the grace God has given me, I laid a foundation as a wise builder, and someone else is building on it. But each one should build with care. For no one can lay any foundation other than the one already laid, which is Jesus Christ. If anyone builds on this foundation using gold, silver, costly stones, wood, hay or straw, their work will be shown for what it is, because the Day will bring it to light. It will be revealed with fire, and the fire will test the quality of each person's work. If what has been built survives, the builder will receive a reward. If it is burned up, the builder will suffer loss but yet will be saved—even though only as one escaping through the flames. (1 Cor. 3:9–15)

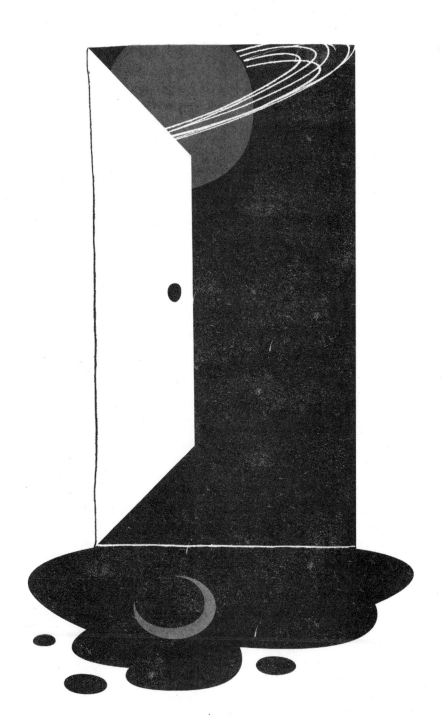

12/15/97 —— STUDY TITLE: "Planning the Unknown"

Old Covenant: Are my plans part of God's purpose? Would God ever ask us to give up the familiar for the unknown?
Jeremiah 29:11; Genesis 12:1

New Covenant: Should I seek God's will when I make plans?
Romans 12:1–2; James 4:13–17

Poetry & Wisdom: Are my passions put in me by God?
Psalm 37:4; Proverbs 27:14   Should I pursue them?

prayer:

Lord, what makes a heart beautiful to you? Faith? Trust? I don't understand your ways, but I am burning in my soul to learn them, because you are good, kind, and holy, and you, God, are love. Apart from you we can do nothing, but with you all things are possible. If trust is beautiful to you, then please, Lord, fill my heart with trust, because I want so much to make myself lovely to you in every way. You have been so much more than kind to me. I love you forever. Amen.

random acts of KINDNESS (RAK) TO-DO:

- ☐ Finish new song "Sacred"
- ☐ Clean kitchen for Granny
- ☐ Hide happy note in sister's backpack
- ☐ Make peach cobbler for neighbors
- ☐ Give Quest Study Bible to Melanie

Song: "Sacred"

Chords: G, G/A, C, G/B, G

Verse: I know it seems like there's nothing sacred anymore
and the world is dark lit up with only flames of war.
It's such an empty place when longing for human praise
they walk away; I'm left wide open and my heart bleeds
and breaks wide open.

Chorus: I hear there's a sacred place, just within heaven's gates
if only heaven's gates were open (x 2)
but all I have is a broken heart and all I do is fall apart
if only heaven's gates were open (x 2)

RECIPE:

Granny's Peach Cobbler

INGREDIENTS:
1 box of yellow cake mix
1 stick (½ cup) of melted butter
(if you don't have squeeze
butter)
1 (29 oz.) can of peaches in heavy
syrup
Lots of sugar. Lots.

DIRECTIONS:
Pour undrained peaches into an 8
or 9 inch square baking pan. Take
a butter knife and cut the peaches
into bite-sized pieces. Put more
sugar in.

Cover peaches with a thin layer
of cake mix. Take your knife and
push some of the cake mix into the
syrup. Cover with another layer
of cake mix. You'll only use about
half of the box. Cover cake mix with
melted butter. (If you can get your
hands on some squeeze butter, then
use that.) Bake at 375°F until it's
golden brown and smells delicious,
about 30–45 min., depending on your
oven. Granny says, "Call your momma
and tell her you love her, and if you
don't straighten up, I'm gonna poke
your eyes out."

PM Through the Bible Reading:

Old Covenant: Deuteronomy 30
New Covenant: Matthew 6
Poetry & Wisdom: Psalm 139

yes
Yes
YES
yes
YES
yes.
yes
YES
yes
YES
yes
yes
YES
YES
yes
yes
yes
yes
YES.

AVAILABLE

RETURNING MY PLANS

Reflection

In the presence of God, any plan that doesn't line up with his own plans turns to ash. The eternal perspective in his presence purifies every human ambition. There is a thankfulness in deep worship that makes us want to open our hands and lift them to heaven.

Open hands are a sign of surrendering and being emptied out before God.

When I move and operate from this place of surrender and emptying, this place of open hands, I find I can be brave enough and "nothing" enough to receive God's plans and power for my life.

How to Become a Bright Light

We had our first snowfall of the season the other day. It was as if God put a fluffy, sparkling, white blanket over the entire wood around us. When I walked outside, the quiet shocked me. It felt like God whispered, *Hush. Listen. Be still.*

And everything obeyed him. It made me want to obey him as well. This is what it feels like to me when seasons change.

The first time I planned to commit suicide I was rescued by an encounter with God. I have lived through many seasons since that day. Every time a new season begins, I feel brand-new somehow. It reminds me of that first morning after being born again.

On the morning after rebirth, I stared at the ceiling in curious awe. I felt like a blank canvas, made to be filled with colors and poetic imagery, all swirling in the mind of the artist who had willed me back to life.

I was a brand-new beating heart before him. After he made me new, the only word I uttered to him was "Yes."

I had no plans. Except to die the night before. Indeed, inwardly, I had.

Now what? My prior life had disintegrated into rich, fertile soil of life-producing death.

What goes through the mind of a newborn baby when she first opens her eyes?

It must be extreme wonder, awe, openness, receptivity, complete humility. Totally vulnerable, dependent on whomever is willing to care. When our hearts say, *I know nothing. God, help*, I believe we have come to a place of new birth, new growth, and a change of season.

Some people take longer to get to this place than others, and so, for some, the seasons are slower to shift.

God's will brings us to life.

He blesses us creatures made in his image with a will of our own.

He made us to be his children, but the unique combination of our minds, wills, and emotions makes us human souls.

I was once speaking to a brilliant and delightful agnostic who said to me, "I look into the face of my daughter, and her innocence, wonder, beauty, and life are so amazing. Don't you think that looking into the face of your child is really like God? Isn't that really what God is, in a way?"

It makes so much sense to me how we come to this thought process, but it's shortsighted.

We can be awed by the God-like beauty in children because God made humans in his image—not the other way around. Perhaps children, new humans with fresh souls, exist in the least-tainted state that humanity can be in, in this life.

How beautiful to see the innocence, wonder, humility, fresh creativity, purity, extreme faith, and freely given love that are so indicative of God's home in heaven and our eternal home that we unconsciously long for it all of our lives here on earth.

Jesus said, "Unless you become like little children, you cannot enter heaven" (see Matt. 18:3).

Maybe we are too "smart" sometimes to let God take us to a new facet of heaven. Maybe we are too proud.

Maybe we are too respectable.

Maybe we are too political or religious.

Maybe we are too focused on our pain or fears.

Maybe we are too controlling.

For some reason, there are times in my life when I use my free will to resist growing in my soul. This is when the season freezes or seems to go backward into some dead, long-gone still frame or rerun in which I know all the lines, blocking, costumes, and jokes. This is when I have ceased to learn. This can become an illusion of security, but there is nothing secure about fear keeping you in a prison of complacency. That's not security; that's just premature, slow death.

I plead with God to make my life into whatever work of art he wants.

My prayer is that I would not become any of these things that would keep me from becoming a bright light, shining with new facets of the wisdom and love of God.

"Of course I'd want to be an actor, but you never know. I make pretty good money at Smokey's. Granted, a barbecue place isn't the best environment for a vegetarian, but I stay in the front making bread and serving ice cream and cobbler. I'll probably go to college and study computers or something though."

I was always fascinated by Cora's personality. So artistic and yet so practical. I could feel it like a cloud: depression. Dark blue-gray, familiar and enticing.

I wanted to disagree with Cora in that moment, for the way she sort of ran her words like a knife through the idea of following her heart or believing in dreams. But I knew that what she was saying sounded a lot like things I had always thought about too. And the cloudy sadness that followed those thoughts was deep and familiar.

But since my encounter with God, I deal with the temptation to wrap up in the familiar comfortable, cold blanket of depression by going off alone with him.

I knew where there was a single-stall bathroom behind the theater stage. When I slipped out of the room I immediately felt the fingers of the cloud trying to wrap around my throat. My tongue began to pray from my spirit by singing heaven songs. Sometimes I make them up. This time I just went through the motions of the first one I could remember:

As the deer pants for the water, so my soul longs after you. You alone are my heart's desire, and I long to worship you.[1]

1. Martin Nystrom, "As the Deer," © 1984 by Maranatha Praise, Inc.

As I sang quietly under my breath, my soul began to respond and demons began to go quiet in my head. I reached the bathroom, fell on my knees, and laid my face on the cold tile.

"I miss you," I told him just before I began to cry.

Worship came from my sobs, and he met me there in that tiny bathroom.

It was like standing at the threshold of a doorway that opens to galaxies spread out before me. Swallowed up by a vertigo of the soul, my body felt weightless.

The surface of my skin was covered in chills. And just beneath, a warm river of light seemed to glow bright, fluidly finding currents down my arms, through my chest, all around my skull, flooding my ears, pouring down along my jawline, tracing my ribs, and pooling deep in my stomach, moving like a sea full of life, covered in winds and magnetized with moon tides.

These are the puny words our English language gives me to describe a glimpse of what it feels like to be filled with the Holy Spirit. This is what it feels like when his Spirit is moving.

There is nothing else like it.

I never thought in these moments, while giving him my full attention, to acknowledge myself. But now, I notice the truth of what a father in the faith said to me once.

"The universe cannot contain God. But he has leaned into your breath, waiting for your invitation for him to live in your heart. You, precious one, must be a lot bigger on the inside than you can even know."

Cavernous. Expansive. Deep. Dense. Rich. Full. Heavy. Open. Wide. Limitless.

Who knew that somehow, within me, a throne room existed, fitting for God? I must be so big inside. And I must be utterly void and formless without God in his rightful place within me.

This must be why nothing has ever fulfilled me that isn't him. This is why I am never satisfied with the shallow answers the world tries to give me for things that seem deeper than anyone is willing to go.

Since I was a child I have wondered about purpose and asked, "Why?" and "What is the point?"

Standing on the edge of life, with God, I know this: Return is the point. Returning to my Creator.

And I want to die to everything else and stay with him. Forever.

Pulling time off your soul feels like taking off shoes that have always been a half size too small. Involuntary sounds of relief escaped my lungs. I didn't realize until then that I had never felt peace or freedom.

Eternity is truly the home of the heart. And I want to stay inside this *forever*.

But God has an order.

God has an adventure planned. For me.

He hasn't taken my breath from this body yet. And he says that this is a good thing for now. When I become aware of God, I know nothing. I have no other words except "Yes, Lord," with all my being. Everything in me says yes because his goodness is so perfect and powerful.

His love is like a black hole pulling everything into his truth, and all that comes out of my soul is yes.

Songs pour from my heart.

There is nothing beyond you, no one like you, nothing I want but you. All I want to do is to say yes to you always.

God interrupted the plan I had for my life. My plan was to die. Suicide was my plan. Back then I had no reverence for my life, my future, my potential, or life's possibilities. So God broke into that moment of barreling toward death and responded to my irreverence by loving me so tangibly that I couldn't want to die anymore.

His kindness is what leads us to true repentance.

His love was so complete and deep and powerful that I would never want to break his heart by hating what he loved so much. I couldn't despise myself anymore. I couldn't be flippant with my life because it was so precious to God.

I know my life is precious to him because that's what I feel when I worship.

So then, kneeling there on the bathroom floor, I asked myself, *What are your plans now?*

Blank canvas life. I was new and full and empty. Over and over my heart sang, *Whatever you want, I want that too. I have no more plans except to say yes to you.*

Open, empty hands.

Everything I have.

All for you, whatever you want to do. Do.

I return my life to you. In you there is no withholding and in you there is no lack. Please take my empty hands in yours.

All I want is to love you back.

Time

Time is a measure
Abstract, it's a number
Created to measure the will
Time unrolls as humans make choices
Time holds death but it doesn't kill

The will of every human measured
Time is the great divine ledger
Our choices becoming a journal
But choices are made in freedom
Freedom, now that is eternal

Time is just a location
Time appears like a fading star
Just a galaxy in the universe of freedom
Unfolding to show who we are
Choices are always alive as
Eternal moments of freedom
The free choice of man will rest or strive
To destroy or restore Eden

But time just measures the will
And when it's done giving its gift
Time will be rolled up and put away
The mere measuring tape that it is

Freedom of choice
Terrifying responsibility and right
Our choices of death are only erased
By the blood of Jesus Christ
He set before us life and death
And pleads for us to choose life
He honors our freedom whatever we choose
But gives us the chance to love right

He chooses the ones who will choose him
And he is both first and last
Our choices are eternal
But Christ's blood rewrites the past

We all have the opportunity
To turn our will toward his
Love him back for his mercy
Believe by his blood he forgives

So choose life or choose death

Come to light or hide in dark
And with every choice you make
Time will measure who you are

God is always speaking
Father of us all
Holy Ghost of Jesus Christ
Calling you, he calls:

"You are the parallel universe
You are the split
In your heart choose life or death
And I will honor it

I am the one
With my blood, who blots out paths of death

But you must choose if you will me to
Or will you keep running ahead?

Yes, parallel universes are possibilities
And they exist within you
And you move back and forth with ease
And enter the futures you choose

Each one is a parallel universe
Eternal souls covered in mud
Freedom is unending parallel universes
And they all intersect with my blood

When each one comes to this crossroad
All wills make a choice
And from these points on, forever
Life or death will have a voice."

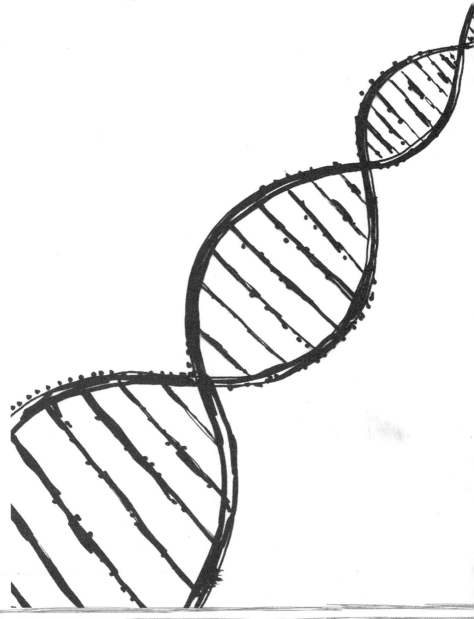

OLD COVENANT: How can I tell where a thought is from?
Genesis 3:1–5; Judges 6:15; Job 33:14

 NEW COVENANT: What do I do with unrighteous thinking?
What does righteous thinking look like?
John 10:10; Revelation 12:10; 2 Corinthians 10:5; Mark 7:21–23; James 4:7;
Galatians 5:22–23; Matthew 4:3–4; Ephesians 6:13–18

POETRY & WISDOM: Since eternity is my destiny, how can I keep an eternal
perspective in this temporary life?
Psalm 139:23; Ecclesiastes 11–12

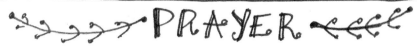

PRAYER

Daddy, thank you for a new day. I just want to walk around in your
mind and see what you're thinking about. Thank you for the Scriptures.
Thank you for how your presence fills the room when I worship you.
Thank you for making yourself known to us. Thank you for giving
humankind purpose—to know and love you and to be known and loved
by you. Let me see others through your eyes. Help me understand your
ways. I invite you to love others through me. Help me to see me the way
you see me. How can I love others as I love myself if I don't love myself?
In the midst of all the temporary things around me, give me eternal
perspective. Your kingdom come and your will be done, in my heart as it
is in heaven. Amen.

 R A K & TO-DO:
♡ Paint my little sister's nails
♡ Write a love song to Jesus
♡ Give <u>Screwtape Letters</u> by C. S. Lewis to Michael
♡ Clean up my room, do laundry, dye my hair
♡ Babysit tonight! Make shepherd's pie for the kids

New Song Idea: "Breath of Eternity"

Verse: D, C2 (pluck verse)
Pre-chorus: D, C2
Chorus: D, C2, D, A, G, A, G, A, D, C2 (strum chorus)

Verse: Seems like I'm always waiting to come back here. When life starts to lead my mind elsewhere, the ache begins low and grows to hunger that I can't control. My soul starts to wonder, where did you go? When did I leave? I didn't mean to, but I always miss you.

Pre-chorus: Breath of Eternity, forever alive in me, hold my thoughts in your strong arms. I bring you my whole life, all I am inside.

Chorus- There's no one more beautiful, there's no love more true than you. I want my whole life to be ceaseless worship to you.

RECIPE: Mom's Shepherd's Pie

INGREDIENTS:
1 lb. ground beef
2 tsp. onion powder
1 tsp. garlic powder
2 tsp. salt
2 tsp. pepper
1 (15 oz.) can of corn, drained
9 slices American cheese
4-6 med. potatoes
1 stick (½ cup) butter
¼ cup milk
2 tbsp. mayonnaise

DIRECTIONS:
Preheat oven to 375°F. Brown ground beef and drain. Add spices. Put in bottom of 9 X 13 casserole pan. Cover beef layer with corn. Cover corn with Mom's mashed potatoes.* Cover mashed potatoes with sliced cheese. Bake until heated through and cheese is melted, about 30-45 min.

*MOM'S MASHED POTATOES
Slice potatoes (peel if desired) and boil until tender (about 10-15 min.). Drain and add butter, milk, and mayo, plus salt and pepper to taste. Mash while still hot. (Use hand mixer for smooth mashed potatoes.)

PM BIBLE READING

OLD COVENANT: Jeremiah 31
NEW COVENANT: Hebrews 10
POETRY & WISDOM: Psalm 73

EPIPHANY

RETURNING MY THOUGHTS

Reflection

The enemy of my soul tries to lie to me every day, wanting to shape my thoughts. Lies like:

> God doesn't love you.
> You are a random clump of cells floating in a universe with no
>   purpose, so make up your own.
> Your body is ugly. Your body is a mistake.
> Other people are your judges, or other people don't matter.

But at the same time the Truth is singing out God's message every day to my soul:

> God loves you.
> You are his artwork.
> God made you on purpose.
> Your body is his art.
> So are others.

His love notes are the beauty around us that extends beyond mere function and necessity: music, laughter, art of all kinds, relationships, and so on.

When we have eyes to see, ears to hear, and a heart to understand how he has drenched the world in his love for us, it will lead us on the adventures he has in mind for us. Seeking these love notes in the world will shift us from control and fear to freedom and faith.

Love Letters from Heaven

The whole world is filled with messages of God's love.

Prayer: Lord, give us eyes to see them, teach our hearts how to understand the language you write your love letters in, in every direction we look, and let our ears hear your whispers of love calling us to rest and grow. Amen.

The wood grain on the coffee shop floor spoke to me today. Counting rings in a stump tells the age of a tree. The wood floors displayed swirls that looked like ripples in water. A water ripple mirrors the effect each life has. The swirls in the wood echo the impact of time on the individual.

Seconds push into hours.

Days.

Years.

Building on each other, impacting the design across the whole board.

Make the most use of every opportunity, he whispers.

The revelation burns my stomach hotter than the mint tea I'm about to dilute with my tears. I blush at the understanding that God is speaking . . . giving me attention.

Butterflies.

The tea. I've been waiting to drink it. It was too hot for me. My friend, on the other hand, gulped down her chai right away, eyes rolling back with pleasure at the fragrant, spicy deliciousness.

"I burned the tip of my tongue trying to drink mine; how'd you just drink it like that?" I asked.

"I dunno." She shrugged. "But it's so good!" She smiled and went back to working on her homework.

I felt his whisper guiding my thoughts to answer my seemingly random musing.

Her capacity is different from yours. Her taste buds are different. Her perspective is different. I made her different. Would it be criminal for her to force you to drink her tea at the temperature she prefers? Your tongue would burn. You'd feel only pain and not be able to taste

any of what she enjoyed when she drank. Do you think the way you spoke to your brother today was too passionate for his taste? Maybe people you love see you as angry.

But I'm not angry, just passionate. My thoughts respond to God in ridiculous defense of the conversation I'd had earlier that caused my brother to leave the room upset.

All he felt was pain. He was unable to hear any of the good things you wanted to say to encourage him. He felt violated. Be patient, cool off a bit, add some honey, and then speak in the right way, at the right time. I know you love him, but he doesn't.

My heart broke at the revelation. I felt alone, misunderstood by people.

As I sat in the coffee shop, I remembered the last time I saw my face, how ugly I felt. I'd caught my reflection in the mirror as I was leaving the house earlier. I looked tired, sad, and lonely. I couldn't remember where I'd put my makeup bag, but my friend was outside, honking for me to come on.

I began to daydream about how to tell the difference between the enemy's voice, my own voice, and the voice of my Creator. There are Scriptures that call Satan the accuser of the brethren and the father of lies, whose goal is to steal, to kill, and to destroy. Certainly these thoughts felt destructive. My own voice tends to sound uncertain. Even in the Scriptures, the people who are called by God tend to doubt themselves. God's Spirit, who speaks to the hearts of his children, is described in the Scriptures as being loving, joyful, peaceful, patient, kind, good, faithful, and gentle.[1]

As I thought through this, the song in the coffee shop changed and a voice rang out, "You . . . are . . . so . . . beautiful . . . to me . . ."

I knew God was singing to me. It melted my heart, and I had to excuse myself to the bathroom to cry. After I closed the door, I stood in

---

1. See Revelation 12:10; John 8:44; 10:10; Galatians 5:22–23.

front of the mirror, studying my face. "You made my face. Let me see me the way you see me," I said to God.

First of all, he whispered, *This body is the beautiful home I've given you, the temple I've made for myself. But your heart is what matters most to me.*

A Scripture rolled across my mind: "People look at the outward appearance, but the Lᴏʀᴅ looks at the heart" (1 Sam. 16:7).

Then another Scripture: "Your adornment must not be merely external—braiding the hair, and wearing gold jewelry, or putting on dresses; but let it be the hidden person of the heart" (1 Pet. 3:3–4 NASB).

Then I heard him whispering again. *You were made in my image. Your heart is beautiful, and that makes your face beautiful.*

He is always whispering. Whispering his love for us.

On the way home, I saw flowers in the midst of rubble at a demolition site. They looked so bright and powerful shooting up out of the dirt with brown debris all around. *I have gifts for you in the middle of the destruction you see in the world. And you are my flower; you are my gift to the world, bright and powerful in the midst of dead, brown chaos.*

I blushed again and felt so loved, pursued, delighted in. I'm a gift.

~eeee **My Body, My Temple** ~eeee~

The rain
On the roof
On the gravel
On the tree branches
On the orange and yellow leaves

The rain
Hitting puddles
Each drop
Its own
Melody:
Its own
Bath
For some square inch
Of earth, or creature
Its own
Calling
Assignment
Journey

Its own longitude and latitude

Rain covering
The roof
In soft melodies
And sadness

Soft sadness
Mixed
With hope
And certainty
The colors
Grey with blue
Purple hues

The pastel brown rivers
Carrying deadness to
Another place
Colorful
Soggy
Deadness

Wet black sticks
Shine bright
Against the gentle amber
All around

And I am dry inside
On my bed
Relishing
The music
Of rain
Inside my head
Feeling
The dampness
On my face
Cooling my hair
My arms
My lips
The corners of
My eyes

The drops join
Together in rivers
Tracing the curves
Of my face
Over my chin
Down my neck
Tickling my collarbone
With romantic playfulness
And adoration
Of how God sculpted me

Making me adore
The way he used
The hands of time
To rework
The lines of my features
Making me
Aware of the beauty
In his architecture

And I,
Along with
The rain
And the heavens
Am thankful
For my own temple's changing

Growing

Fading
Shifting physical beauty

Like an outdoor shower
Of thankfulness
And wonder
I lie in the dark room
Dry and warm
Feeling the music
Of the heavenly waters
Kissing my skin
Kissing
My clothes
Dotting a bright red jacket
With dark red round evidence
Of our dance
Together,
The jacket itself,
Love and hospitality

My knitted cap
Crowning my head
Gently
Kindly
A gift
Of bright orange hope
Made by a woman
Who escaped abuse in Uganda
Was paid well for her audacity
To believe that she could build a new life
One bright orange stitch at a time

And the delicate embrace she has knit for
   my heavy head
Lifts the weight off me with a dizzying,
   glorious, aching hope

The beauty
Of the harsh world
Can arise again
With the softest acts
Of hope

The softness hugs me when I feel
Neglected
And in need
Of physical touch

The hat and jacket hold me
They rejoice with me
As I continue
To dance
In the rain
In my mind
Warm and dry
In my bed

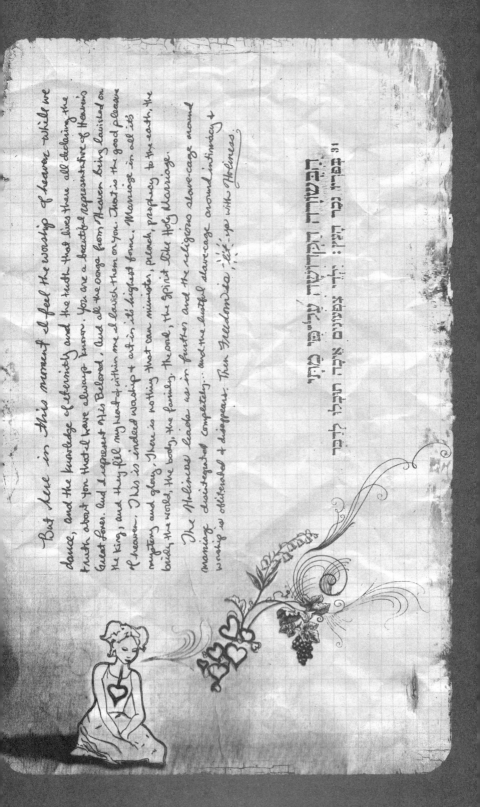

But here in this moment I feel the worship of heaven while we dance, and the knowledge of eternity and the truth that lives there all declaring the truth about you that I have always known. You are a beautiful representative of Heaven's Great Lover. And I represent His Beloved. And all the ways from Heaven being lavished on the king, and they fill my heart within me I lavish them on you. That is the good pleasure of heaven. This is indeed worship + art in its highest form. Marriage in all its mystery and glory. There is nothing that can minister, preach, prophesy to the earth, the bride, the world, the body, the family, the throne, the Spirit like Holy Marriage.

The Holiness leaks us in fruition and the religious slave-cage around marriage disintegrated completely... and the beautiful slave-cage around intimacy + worship is obliterated + disappears. Then Freedom is "lit-up with Holiness."

16 מַלְאָךְ כֵּן יָצָא : יְתָן הָעַצְמוֹ אֲשֶׁר בַּהֵם בָּכָה
יְהָמוּנוּ יְהָלֵּךָ אֲבֶר בָּבֵר

Old Covenant: Is what I have right in front of me enough?
Genesis 39:20–23; 2 Kings 4:2–7; Zechariah 4:10

New Covenant: What good is it to spend our energy
taking care of little things?
Luke 16:10; Colossians 3:23–24; Romans 12:6–8

Poetry & Wisdom: What am I to do if the little I offer
turns into greatness?
Esther 4:6–17; Revelation 4:10–11

PRAYER

Father, thank you for a new day. Thank you for a bed to sleep in.
Thank you for clothes to wear. Lord, let me have a thankful heart.
Let me have eyes that notice all the goodness and blessings that are
right in front of me. There is always something to thank you for.
Thank you for the opportunities you give us every day to learn more
about you and your love. Help me to shine your love into the world
however I can. Help me to keep my eyes in yours as I do. Thank you for
your love that makes me brave and for how you rescued me. Thank
you that from now on into eternity I can sing about your love forever.
Amen.

RAK & TO-DO:

☐ Practice song for school club performance
☐ Make chicken pillows for movie night with Dee
☐ Give The Robe by Lloyd C. Douglas to Michael
☐ Help little brother with homework
☐ Clean car out for Gramps

New Song Idea: "Christmas Song"

Em, C, G, D (pluck for verse, strum for chorus)

Verse 1: A frightened virgin teenage girl receives a message that defies the laws of this world. All she can do is weep and nod; she's to bring into this world the Son of God.

Chorus: God's angels sound their trumpets and blow their horns. Tonight the long awaited Savior's to be born, the goodness bound by Satan has been torn. With this baby's precious brow ready for thorns.

Verse 2: A star appears fulfilling ancient prophecy; there's an ounce of fear as wise men follow faithfully. The virgin Mary brings forth a human savior, and this future king sleeps soundly in a manger. Tonight he is born, so one day he can die. To heal hearts that are torn and live a perfect life. So he can hang upon a cross and we can take his life, so we can live as sinners and he can pay the price. Tonight he is born so one day he can die. But he will rise again!

RECIPE Aunt Jacky's Chicken Pillows

INGREDIENTS:
- 1 (10 oz.) can of chicken
- ½ (10.5 oz.) can of cream of chicken soup
- 1 (8 oz.) can of crescent roll dough

DIRECTIONS:
Preheat oven according to crescent roll package instructions. Mix together canned chicken and half of the can of cream of chicken soup in a medium bowl. Unroll crescents on a baking sheet. Spoon about 1 tbsp. of chicken mixture onto each crescent triangle. Roll up and bake as directed on the crescent package. Enjoy!

PM THROUGH THE BIBLE READING:

Old Covenant: Genesis 41
New Covenant: Acts 16
Poetry & Wisdom: Job 1

3

GOD TOUCHED

RETURNING MY OPPORTUNITIES

Reflection

This new creature I've become is a soul that's never full. So I open God's love letter. And I read. It's daily bread to my heart.

I feel his breath wrapped up in the letters and his heartbeat just beyond my words. I see him searching me as I take in the message. He has a knowing joy in his eyes—an excitement for me to understand his ways.

The peace, wisdom, and echo of it spreads through me like it has entered my bloodstream. All of it, like a gas stove being turned on, pushing out iridescent swirling shimmers into the air, clicking, clicking, clicking. And here comes the spark:

Well done, good and faithful servant! You have been faithful with a few things; I will put you in charge of many things. Come and share your master's happiness! (Matt. 25:21)

My heart is set ablaze by this Scripture.

The question pounds in my heart: Is this a secret answer to the question I have begged to know?

How can I ever thank God and love him back?

> Is this the secret to touching his heart with my life? Could I possibly bring him joy and share in his joy by being faithful with the few things he's entrusted to me? So I flip to the back of my Bible and look up the word *faithful*. This is where I start my journey of learning more about loving God back.
>
> We can never repay God. But as we catch glimpses of his great love for us, we can't help but want to love him back.

Trying to Touch God

Whenever I pick up my guitar, I always remember the first time I realized I could touch God with music. I was sixteen years old. I picked up my guitar hoping it would become my very own portal to heaven.

I turned on my CD player and listened to a song on the *Passion Worship* CD that a friend had given me. I listened and figured out the root notes to the chords they were playing, and since I had learned guitar because of the punk/grunge scene, I knew how to play a bar chord better than anything else.

As long as I could figure out a way to sing along, it didn't matter to me if it was perfect, because I was only using my guitar like a vehicle to carry my heart to God.

In my encounters with God through worship and through Bible reading, I got the sense my heart was the most important thing to him. Once I memorized the chords and they became a muscle memory in my hands, I closed my eyes and began to sing with my heart.

My voice opened up naturally because my soul was behind it. I wasn't trying to sound pretty; I was just trying to make sure my heart was honest—that whatever I sang, I meant it. And as soon as I made it to this place of honesty, I was no longer alone in my room. I was alone in heaven with God.

Now, there are people all over the world from many different generations who say they have seen heaven and been with God, or Jesus, and seen him face-to-face. I love these stories, and my heart burns whenever I feel like I can tell they truly had an encounter with him like this. But my encounter here was less of an outward experience and more like getting caught up in an amazing book or a dance. I was vaguely aware of still sitting on the floor with a guitar in my hands. But my heart was ascending while it bowed low before my Creator.

It's like releasing everything else that would occupy your thoughts or soul and focusing all your energy on simply knowing that God is *God*. As I sang, I became aware of a story unfolding in my heart. It was about my brother and me. It was a song of freedom that would come in the future, to both our souls, through the love and miracles of God.

I kept playing until the story was clear enough that I would not forget it if I stopped the music to write it down. Then I grabbed my notebook. I scribbled furiously, trying to transpose my thoughts into a language that could capture the hopeful storyline that had gone through me.

Two hours later I could close my eyes, get lost, and play the whole story of our salvation from darkness to light. I cried as I sang and thanked God. It was as if he had accepted my puny offering of a few chords and my heart and given me a song to sing that was on his mind.

The next day during lunch my art teacher sat down right next to me. She smiled and searched my eyes for a minute like she was holding a secret in.

"Lacey, I heard that you play guitar and sing. Is that right? Well, the students who get together in the band hall every Tuesday during lunch have been looking for someone to play guitar and sing some songs for them. Would you want to sing for them?"

Maybe the song I wrote last night was for this group of kids.

"What do they meet in the band room for?"

"They started a Christian Life Club. I'm sure you could ask them about joining if you were interested."

She winked at me.

I knew she wasn't supposed to talk to me about faith, but I guess the rumor had gotten around to the teachers that I had become a Christian. Before that I think I had been on some kind of "watch list." I laughed and told her I'd be there the next day and would bring my guitar.

To my surprise, when I got there the band room was completely full. People were huddled in the open doorway because there wasn't enough room for anyone else to come in.

I had no idea there were so many Christians in my school.

I sat up against a wall on a chair, holding my guitar and waiting for someone to speak up and lead and tell me when to start.

Right at my feet was a pretty punk rock girl with writing all over her mismatched Converse shoes that were falling apart. She had twenty necklaces on and dozens of bracelets on each arm. She was laughing and talking to her friends like she was the happiest girl in the world.

I felt drawn to her, but not because she seemed happy. For some reason I kept thinking that she was sad.

Finally, the room went quiet as the boy leading the meeting introduced me as a special guest with a song for everyone and said he hoped that they liked it. He turned to me and I smiled.

Saying in my head, *I just hope God likes it,* I started the chords like I had in my room. I played them awkwardly over and over, ignoring the room, until I found myself lost again with God, who wanted to sing this story through my voice.

When the song ended, I opened my eyes and the punk rock girl with the mismatched shoes was quietly sobbing. Her shoulders shook while her friends put their arms around her to comfort her.

I marveled at what God could be telling her. I prayed that she would know how much he loved her.

And I shuddered in my soul a little. That wasn't my goal.

I wasn't trying to touch people.

I was trying to touch God.

And somehow, this connected someone to God's heart. Just through an imperfect song played through a novice guitar player and mediocre singer.

This was the first time I saw the miracles God could do with my puny offerings when my motives were all about touching him and no one else.

So I decided to keep offering. Whether I was alone in my room, with my family cleaning the kitchen after dinner, in class at school, waiting tables at Shoney's, or playing at a coffee shop in front of strangers, I could always find something to offer. I could always find some way to love God back. Not so he would love me, but because he loved me already.

As long as I knew God's love and forgiveness were free gifts that I could never earn or pay for, I couldn't help but want to bring back to him all the offerings and sacrifices of love I could.

Today read: 1 Peter 4:8–11

> Above all, love each other deeply,
> because love covers over a multitude of sins.
> Offer hospitality to one another without grumbling.
> Each of you should use whatever gift you have received to
>   serve others,
> as **faithful stewards** of God's grace in its various forms.
> If anyone speaks, they should do so as one who speaks the
>   very words of God.
> If anyone serves, they should do so with the strength God
>   provides, so that in all things God may be praised through
>   Jesus Christ.
> To him be the glory and the power for ever and ever. Amen.

What did God give me?

> For God so loved the world that he gave his only begotten Son,
> that whosoever believes in him should not perish, but have ev-
> erlasting life. (John 3:16 KJV 2000)

God gave us his love.
God gave us himself.

Jesus said, "If you have seen the Son you have seen the Father. I
and my Father are one and the same" (see John 14:9).
Jesus said, "If you love me, you will obey my commands" (see v. 15).
What did he command?
That we "love one another" as he loved us.

He said the greatest commandment is to love the Lord your God with all your heart, with all your soul, with all your mind, and with all your strength. And the second, he said, is like it: love your neighbor as yourself (see Matt. 22:37–39).

So how can I be faithful to love God and people with the few things in front of me?

How do I steward this life I've been given and love God back?

What opportunities are in front of me?

> - SCHOOL
> - WORK
> - HOME
> - SCHOOL CLUBS
> - CHURCH

What gifts have I been given?

What can I do?

> - BABYSIT   - SING   - PAINT
> - WAIT TABLES   - WRITE POETRY   - CLEAN
> - PLAY GUITAR   - JOURNAL   - MAKE FOOD
> - WRITE SONGS   - DRAW   :)

What can I do? Do I have any talents?

Well, I guess I can play the guitar a little. I like to watch kids. I love my job at Shoney's. I love to write poems and journal. I like writing songs. I hate cleaning the kitchen.

Right now? My guitar is just staring at me.

Well, I guess I'll just start here.

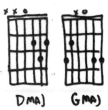

D MAJ   G MAJ

Hungry

I'm awake.
I'm hungry.
So I roll over and eat.
The words are life-giving.
I'm thirsty.
The truths are living water.
I drink.
Every morning is the same.
Every morning is new.

is god
REAL?
DOES
HE
care
?

9/4/99 Study Title: "Eternal Perspective = Purity"

Old Covenant: Do God's ways always make sense to the human mind?
1 Samuel 16:7; Isaiah 55:8–9

New Covenant: Ultimately, is our struggle in life against other people, or something else? Are Christians free to sin because of grace? What is love?
Ephesians 6:12; Galatians 5:13; 1 Corinthians 4–6

Poetry & Wisdom: Are earthly rewards and perspectives satisfying?
Ecclesiastes 11:8–21; 12:8, 13–14

PRAYER

Daddy, you are so kind. You see everything and your love reaches everyone, and all who love truth find you. I see all these people sitting in their own hatred like there is nowhere else to go. Thank you, Lord, for being the way, the gate by which we come to life and purpose. You love all people; if only we would love you back, we would become fully alive in that love now and forever! The world only gives shallow, fleeting shadows of love, but in you is love true and everlasting. Help me never to abuse my freedom by using it to run away from you or your ways. Your ways truly are the best ways. Deliver me from all the traps of the enemy and take all the condemnation or judgment out of my heart. Let me see like you and love like you. Thank you for helping me find health in my soul and my mind. Help me find health in my body too. You're such a good Daddy. Amen.

RANDOM ACTS OF KINDNESS & TO-DO:

- [ ] Practice for coffee shop
- [ ] Make chicken pot pie for practice
- [ ] Give <u>Till We Have Faces</u> by C. S. Lewis to Airic
- [ ] Clean house for Mom
- [ ] Take little sister to mall

New Song Idea: "Penholder"

Verse: Em, D, C, B · Pre-chorus: C, Bm · Chorus: Em, C, G, D

Verse: I feel your eyes crawling over me, like I'm something more than me, but I don't have anything good enough to say, I just held the pen that day.

Pre-chorus: I'll show you what he did, but I won't take the credit. It's not mine anyway, I just held the pen that day.

Chorus: I don't deserve this, this time right now, it's not something for which I can take the bow. I don't deserve this, it wasn't me, I won't take glory for something that I can't be. I don't deserve this.

RECIPE

Grandma Dorothy's Chicken Pot Pie

INGREDIENTS:
1 cup (8 oz.) canned chicken
1 (10.5 oz.) can of cream of chicken soup
1 (16 oz.) can of mixed veggies
1 cup pancake mix
½ cup milk
1 egg
1 tbsp. bacon bits
shredded cheddar cheese

DIRECTIONS:
Preheat oven to 400°F. Mix chicken, soup, and veggies together in a 9-inch pie pan. In a medium bowl, mix pancake mix, milk, egg, bacon bits , and cheese together until batter is smooth. Pour batter over chicken mixture and bake for 30 min. or until top turns brown.

P.M. BIBLE READING

Old Covenant: Isaiah 6
New Covenant: Revelation 12
Poetry & Wisdom: Psalm 90

SPRING

RETURNING MY PERCEPTIONS

Reflection

When you think of spring, what pops into your mind?

Cool rain showers? New growth pushing through the soil? Cool evenings, warm days? The cold of winter giving way to new life?

Our relationship with God is like spring.

Once we perceive and acknowledge God's love, security takes hold of our hearts. Identity, settled. We are his beloved ones. Our old perceptions pass away. Our old judgments? They give way to a special kind of heavenly rejoicing in all those we see and encounter in this life. Our hearts move from withholding love from others—from judging others—to viewing everyone as God's unique gift to this world.

We can rejoice in his love for us and those around us. Even people we wouldn't notice before or have written off for one reason or another.

We can settle down into the peace he carries as the good and sovereign ruler of the universe. We can trust he will defend us.

We can enjoy life as it changes and know that there's purpose in it all, and it will all work together for good.

Life Chasers

Is God real? Does he care? Will he bring justice? Is he merciful? Is he kind? Is he all-powerful? All-knowing? All-good? I believe the shortest and most profound answer to all these questions is yes.

> Man does not see what the LORD sees, for man sees what is visible, but the LORD sees the heart. (1 Sam. 16:7 HCSB)

> Boast no more so very proudly, do not let arrogance come out of your mouth; for the LORD is a God of knowledge, and with Him actions are weighed. (1 Sam. 2:3 NASB)

> There is a way that seems right to a man,
> but its end is the way to death. (Prov. 14:12 HCSB)

> You intended to harm me, but God intended it for good to accomplish what is now being done, the saving of many lives. (Gen. 50:20)

> We know that all things work together for the good of those who love God: those who are called according to His purpose. (Rom. 8:28 HCSB)

My ability to judge righteously is severely limited.

Human perspective is limited, but my human faith is not. I can *choose* to trust. From a place of pain, trust is miraculous. Humans are meant to be miraculous in the face of the fallen nature that leads to death all around us.

I want to be a miraculous human, in light of the miraculous human Jesus modeled for humanity. He believes in me. He believes in us.

What if everything we thought was wrong in the world was actually God honoring our freedom?

And even when we break the world and each other with our freedom, he touches us in spite of ourselves and shows a holy mercy. Writing morals to every story, covering our recklessness with sober purpose.

Like a master painter who knows how to turn it all into beauty but waits on our invitation.

And for those left in the lurch, impacted by the violence of death and darkness and rebellion?

He notices these disregarded ones with deep compassion.

He turns the invisible into his most profound messengers to the world. He prophesies through them about how light illuminates darkness. They shine to us as a holy kindness meant to lead us all to repentance—to turn us from complacency to responsibility. From death-seeking and death-bringing to life-chasing and life-giving.

Gifts

All life is a gift.

What would happen if we honored the gift of life all around us?

What does it look like to take care of, or steward, this gift of life in us and all around us? When you are loved so deeply, the natural response is to love back, to be thankful. What does it look like to love back? To be thankful?

Only one more year left of high school. Today I felt the weight of having hardly any time left to love the people here. I wish I could have known them all. They are all so important, but not many of them know it. Today I saw this in living color walking in the hall between classes.

I heard someone say, "What a waste of space."

I turned just in time to see a girl push another girl out of the way. The girl being pushed held her glasses in place and tried to ignore the hateful moment.

"What are you looking at with your stupid glasses?" the accuser said, glancing in my direction just enough for me to see the hatred in her eyes.

I was amazed to feel myself fill up with a weight of sadness and compassion for this "enemy."

I would have gotten into a cussing fight with her before I met God. And now I realized that her accusation was not against me or the girl she pushed at all. It was against our maker. And God is so powerful and beautiful. He can defend himself if he wants. If he does not, it must be grace, giving us time to come to our senses.

I was sad that she couldn't have joy over the gift of life that God had put in her and all around her. My heart broke over them both. The one who had such hate in her heart. Poisoning her soul and killing her spirit.

I wondered where she learned to treat people that way. I wondered about her hidden pain that had somehow turned to such a calloused way to carry herself.

My heart broke over the girl she had pushed. This girl expected life to treat her the way she was just treated. Always finding scenarios that seemed to support the lie she believed about herself: that she was worthless.

I related to both girls.

If only they knew that you created us with love and care. If only they knew that we are all your art, I said to God. Our conversation went deeper.

If we are all your art, what are the disregarded ones saying about who you are? I asked him in my restlessness over what the world calls "handicaps."

Come and see, he whispered.

So I asked the special education teacher if I could spend my lunch in the special ed. room. I could see God's fingerprints on her immediately when she smiled. Her joy and peace were beautiful in a whimsical, artistic way.

Acceptance. Presence. Pure Joy. Be.

Lunchtime came, and as I walked to the special education classroom, I was a little nervous over what I might experience. So I was delighted to find such a unique facet of glory hidden away in the back room of the school building.

When I came through the door, I was immediately drawn to a very large boy with a tangled mess of brown hair.

His eyes seemed to roam back and forth, seeing nothing. His head waved back and forth like a flag in a soft breeze.

Is he blind? I asked God.

Watch, he answered.

He looked blind, sitting on his own, alone in a corner, in his own world.

He isn't alone, whispered God to my thoughts.

Then I noticed Bach, quietly soaring through the room.

Perhaps he is being the violin. I smiled, noticing now that he seemed to be moving in time with the melody.

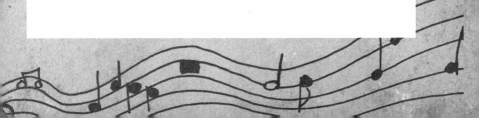

Music can be loved by us, but it can't love us back. Music makes us feel less alone, but it isn't the true source of company.

It's you, isn't it? I asked God, wondering if he meant that the boy wasn't alone because God was with him.

Yes. I sensed God's great love for him. Everywhere he goes he is like a flashlight revealing the true heart of men.

I shuddered at what light does to us when we are hiding pride, sin, selfishness, or superiority in our hearts.

It's humiliating. We run. We ignore, and stammer, and justify, and look for cover so we won't be found out.

Let me never be afraid of your light, I prayed.

Then I saw that he wasn't blind. His teacher walked over, singing his name.

"Brandon the biggest, Brandon the great; oh, how I'd love to see your face."

He doesn't seem to notice her song as she walks over to him. She takes his head in her hands and turns it gently so that he can be still, and face her, and see her.

In this still moment, his eyes ever so slightly slow down.

He *sees* her.

You can feel the light spread through him when he does, and his smile changes ever so slightly into something different. He has been hit by her love. Warm in his ears, maybe, and that's why he grabs them, and warm in his belly, maybe, and that's why he pushes out a shout of joy from his diaphragm, loud and boisterous and, when you are paying attention, so beautiful you want to laugh with him.

Like watching a bud you thought was just a plant turn into a flower right in front of your eyes. His joy, so pure.

He is present and the world doesn't distract him.

This is what Brandon says about God.

He is acceptance.

Like a leaf blowing in the wind, a message of peace.

This is what Brandon preaches to us.

Be still. Just be.

I want to clap for him and clap for God for thinking of a way to teach the world what pure acceptance and pure presence look like. I love him. I will think of him when my soul starts to strive. I will think of him when I'm distracted and I know that God is ever so slightly turning my head in his hands, singing over me about how he loves to see my face.

I will pray for myself.

Father, help me to honor the message you are speaking through those around me. I realize that if I don't look to find you in others, I will rob myself of knowing you fully.

~~~~~ Numb ~~~~~

Being numb
Is like overheating.
Like your heart
Stopping
Because it was beating too fast.
It's all
Too much;
Eventually the tattooing,
Scraping,
Burning,
Slicing
Into your souls
Leaves scar tissue;
Unfeeling.

Numb.

But still
Uncomfortably achy.

"A man walks into a brothel looking for God."

We search
So long
For the itch to scratch
So we can rest
But we live
Blistered and bleeding,
Scratching everywhere,
Looking
For our souls
On the surface
Of our skin.

Our eyes
Pushed out by two unmerciful feet,
Unrelenting;
The pressure.

Our minds
Ooze out of our ears;
We desire
The euphoria, the eureka,
The philosophical highs
That made us feel
Above them all
Above
Our former selves.

Exhausted,
We ache all over,
And where is the soul?

Lost
Dark
Dying
Starving
Abused
Neglected
Panting for God.

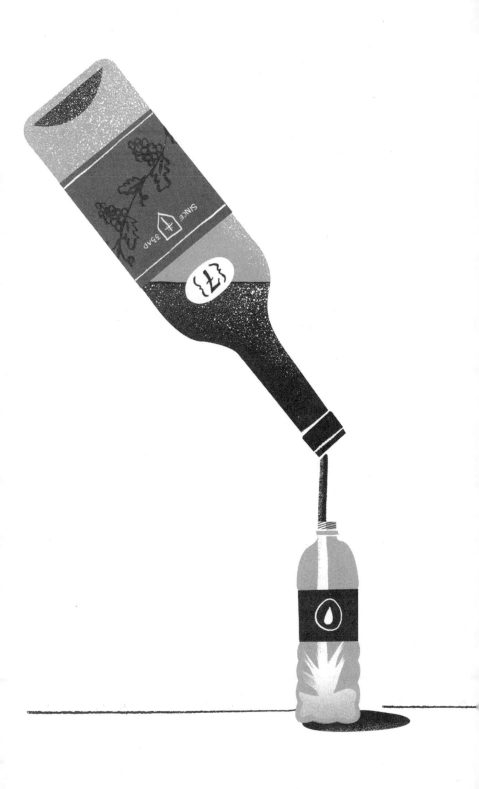

7/14/02   Study Title: "No Slave to Desire"

Old Covenant: Does Jesus know what it's like to be sad? How can we guard our hearts from lust?   Isaiah 53:3; Job 31:1

New Covenant: Can we make the Holy Spirit sad? Is it good to act like animals or like we are governed or enslaved by instinct? Should we relax about sin?
        Ephesians 4:30; Jude 1:10; Galatians 5:1; Matthew 5:30; 1 Corinthians 15:33–34

Poetry & Wisdom: Do our souls boss us arounz, or do we parent our souls? Should we be friends with lust?   Psalm 43:5; Proverbs 5:3–8

PRAYER

Thank you, Father, for the way you invite us in. The enemy says, "Do this, do this, do this," and then he says, "How could you do that? You are worthless." And you say, "Look in my eyes. I can turn this into glory if you let me clean you off and help you up. But you have to turn around, quit going that way, and look at me. I love you. Let me help." Lord, make me brave enough to come into the light and not hide in shame in the dark. Let me be brave enough to hand you everything. I trust you. Amen.

RAK & To-Do:
- [ ] Make guacamole and black bean dip for band practice
- [ ] Weed Jamie's purple iris flower beds
- [ ] Give <u>Wild at Heart</u> to Lee
- [ ] Call little brother Phillip and check on him

New Song Idea: "Sleepwalker"

F, Am, G

Verse: My spirit is willing, but my flesh is weak; my eyelids grow heavy, and I might just fall asleep. How many times will I go and take the bait only for this hook to rip right through my face?

Chorus: How can I love you back? What can I do to show you? His piercing eyes meet mine. Please simply stay awake. Talk to me and I'll hear you. Don't fall asleep this time; gotta stay awake, gotta stay awake.

RECIPE: GUACAMOLE

INGREDIENTS:

4-6 pitted, peeled, and mashed avocados

1 cup chopped red bell pepper, 1 cup chopped orange bell pepper, ½ cup chopped green bell pepper, ½ cup quartered cherry tomatoes

1 tsp. garlic powder or 2 cloves minced garlic, ½ cup chopped fresh cilantro, 1½ tsp. cumin, juice of 1 lime

DIRECTIONS:

Mix all ingredients together. (For easier guacamole, just mix mashed avocado with your favorite salsa and lime juice.)

RECIPE:
Easy Black Bean Dip

Blend equal amounts canned black beans (drained and rinsed) and salsa in blender till smooth.

(Add juice of 1 lime, 1 tsp. cumin, 1 tsp. salt, and a handful of chopped cilantro to blender if desired.)

PM Through the Bible Reading:

Old Covenant: 2 Samuel 13
New Covenant: John 8
Poetry & Wisdom: Proverbs 7

4.267.330.47 2:17A.M.

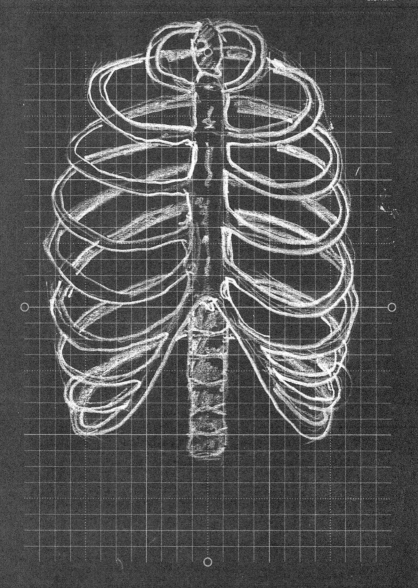

STOUT INSTITUTE OF RESEARCH & DEVELOPMENT

GRAVITY CAGE

RETURNING MY BODY, SEXUALITY & SOUL

Reflection

We thirst for life. We thirst for death. And we stand confused about it all. You, oh God, made us. Carved us in the mud—scraping us together. You breathed into us. So I know everything in me is from you. And yet, I battle. Wrestling with that one called the liar.

He twists everything. He's a twister. A tornado of lies.

He accuses my body—and speaks lies about it.

He accuses my passions—and whispers sweet nothings about them.

He accuses my sexuality—and tries to abuse and warp my vision of it.

He attempts to wring my soul dry . . . with lies.

But I can hear you, Lover of my soul. And you say, "I have told you these things, so that in me you may have peace. In this world you will have trouble. But take heart! I have overcome the world" (John 16:33).

Sucked into Gravity and Time

We are not animals, and we must stop talking about ourselves and our fellow humans as though we are. It's much better to say what Jesus said in John 10:34 when he quoted David in Psalm 82:6, that we are God's little gods. God's children—his own offspring made.

In his image, we look much less like animals than we do like gods behaving like animals at times.

We become fallen gods when we act like animals.

Demonic creatures.

We are not addicted rats that keep ringing a bell for an orgasm till we die; we are gods who make romantic sexuality sacred and tear up over the miracle of withholding and making this event a shared gift for the right time with the right person.

We weep because God weeps.

We laugh because our heavenly Father does.

The distinction we have from animals is significant in a magnificent way, in a godly way. For we are his little gods, made in his image to do good works he planned in advance for us to do with the most godlike of our qualities: our free will.

He gives us choice because he makes choices. It is in this that we glow with the utmost God-ness, because it is only with choice that we are able to love in divine ways.

We must *stop* referencing love the way we reference animalistic addiction. When we lose the choice to love, we have only become addicts, jumping from one addiction to the next according to how good it makes us "feel." But we, who are created in the image of God, are made to house the Holy Spirit of God within us, and he empowers us to make covenants and keep them as our heavenly Father does. We can make choices to lay down our lives for love's sake, and this is the greatest and godliest of our abilities. We are God's kids, and we prove it when we divinely sacrifice for love more than any other time.

Godly Sorrow

Sadness is not always a bad thing. Sometimes sadness is indicative of a heart of compassion. Love can be sad sometimes. Sadness is even godly at times.

Jesus was called a man of sorrows.[1]

The Bible says that God's Holy Spirit can be grieved by the things we do. This makes me want to weep, because I know I have done this before to my Lord, my King, my Savior, my heavenly Father, my True Love. I have grieved his Spirit. Because he loves me. Because he has bled and died to make his home within me, and I have done things in this house of God that are hurtful to my humble, gentle, just, merciful, and all-powerful Lord and Savior.

How can such a holy, awesome God tolerate a home where sin invades, sometimes willingly, by his bride, his host, his roommate, his partner? Because there exists, outside of space and time, the crucified Christ, crucified from creation, who suffered once and for all for my sins, past, present, and future.

All sin exists outside of space and time. All sin is cosmic treason against the holy God who created all of us to be his bride, his lover, his temple. When the revelation comes that I have sinned against my only True Love, the grief overwhelms me.

Sorrow that is godly is different from sorrow that is worldly.[2] It leads to change and life. Worldly sorrow leads to self-loathing and death.

Sometimes we must push through our worldly sorrow to get to the godly sorrow, because our pride is ugly and pitches terrible fits before we reach godly sorrow. Our pride has to die, and it is a lying fighter. But as it dies, hope returns. We have nothing left to hold us back and we stand up from the tear-soaked floor we were lying on with nothing to lose, openhanded with our lives and with a heart that says, *I'm all yours. I owe you everything. Here I am, Lord, to die for you, but more importantly to live for you.*

1. Isaiah 53:5.
2. 2 Corinthians 7:10.

Lust /ləst/ *noun* 1. A demon that seeks to pervert the sacredness of sexuality by suggestions in the heart or mind, using words, images, etc. to arouse sexual desire that would attempt to violate your own self-control, to push you into entertaining thoughts or actions that you later regret, not because of religious guilt but because you feel as though lust itself has violated you almost against your free will, much like any addiction. Not to be confused with love, which honors free will.

In Matthew 5:28 Jesus said, "But I tell you that anyone who looks at a woman lustfully has already committed adultery with her in his heart."

There was no image. Not in front of my eyes anyway. It was in my head. An image I had forgotten about and wished away because of how it felt like my dead self. But I was drifting off to sleep when it appeared. Words I'd read painted the image into a scene I could walk right into.

Lust is like an ex-boyfriend, one you loathe the sight of but who speaks in a voice that makes you forget all your convictions. A voice you once could not resist. Here, where lust shows up like an ex-boyfriend for the first time since you fell in love with Someone else, the clarity that came with your new Love makes you wonder how you ever could have fallen for such a liar as your ex. In the midst of his velvet voice, you tell your own voice to obey you and you speak. You tell the alluring liar he is not invited.

But he notices your voice isn't confident. He begins breaking into your house, with a smile of victory, like he's already won. This smile of his makes you want to cry

because you start to believe him instead of yourself. His confidence intimidates you.

This is how I felt. I asked the image to go away, but it grew more colorful and began to come to life. And I felt my will slowly shift into the powerless animal instinct that overtakes your senses. I gave in to the pressure of the demonic weight in the room, ill equipped at the time to fight for my own heart. Like a zombie attack, that old enslaved person I was before I met and fell in love with God had become animated, trying to convince me that I was not really the "new creation in Christ" that I know I really have become.

After the rush of my dead soul coming back to life faded, the demon of lust invited the demons of accusation, condemnation, and shame to bludgeon my heart with self-loathing. This familiar feeling of self-hate was not alluring to me for one second. I recognized this death for the hell that it was right away and cried out to my Savior.

Immediately, I felt his presence. Recognizing him with me—such purity in his presence, such grace and mercy and unconditional love that it crumpled my whole body into a heap on the floor with sobs of sorrow for what had just happened in my heart without him. I couldn't breathe, completely arrested by the revelation of what a constant perfect, holy, just, and merciful God he is.

I was captured by a love that set me free. He came to my wrists, ankles, and neck and broke every chain, and as he did this I clung to his beautiful feet and told him I was his forever. A slave by choice. Love had captured me. Freedom had arrested me. Grace had brought me to justice.

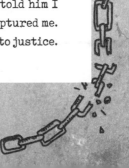

Nothing is worth forgetting what he's done for me . . . and yet the world's minuscule counterfeits can somehow sneak up on us, pulling our gaze away from the colors of the galaxies we are journeying toward to a flickering dollar store flashlight in the corner of a prison cell.

C. S. Lewis described the way we rob ourselves this way: "It would seem that Our Lord finds our desires not too strong, but too weak. We are half-hearted creatures, fooling about with drink and sex and ambition when infinite joy is offered us, like an ignorant child who wants to go on making mud pies in a slum because he cannot imagine what is meant by the offer of a holiday at the sea. We are far too easily pleased."[3]

Recognizing that God has offered us freedom and we've settled for prison—or that he has offered us the ocean and we've settled for mud pies in a slum—can make us sober sometimes with a godly sadness. It is a sort of lovesick heart toward purity. It makes us sad because we sense our complete inability to ever pay back the God who gives all things to us, who loves us with a purity we can never hold on to in and of ourselves. How do we ever love him back?

There is a sadness of wanting to give him more than we have to give, because he deserves all we have left to give and more. He is worth it all and more. He is worthy. It is the sadness of gratitude. The sadness of longing to be closer than we can be. In the Scriptures, the apostle Paul talked about this longing in Philippians 1:23, a longing to die with lovesickness for God, wanting to depart this world and be with Jesus.

3. C. S. Lewis, *The Weight of Glory: And Other Addresses* (New York: HarperCollins, 2001), 26.

JOURNAL—7/14/02

For several decades, we psychologists looked upon the whole matter of sin and moral accountability as a great incubus and acclaimed our liberation from it as epic making. But at length we have discovered that to be free in this sense, that is to have the excuse of being sick rather than sinful, is to court the danger of also becoming lost. . . . We have cut the very roots of our being, lost our deepest sense of self-hood and identity. . . . We find ourselves asking, "Who am I? What is my deepest destiny? What does life mean?"

O. Hobart Mowrer[4]

While eating lunch with a group of people the other day, I ended up in a conversation with my friend Joycie's cousin. He's a handsome guy, with a gift of influence. I was telling Joycie how sad it is that we often think it's impossible to overcome certain sins.

I said, trying to explain what I meant, "Recently, I was completely shattered. I found this horrible part of myself that I didn't think was a big deal. When I prayed about it, I could feel God's heart break over it. I could feel him grieving. There's nothing more devastating than feeling God grieve. It's like seeing my Gramps cry. I mean, if you knew you were breaking the heart of someone you loved, someone who loved you so much, who gave everything for you and wanted nothing but the best for you, wouldn't you do whatever you could to stop bringing him grief?"

This is when Joycie's cousin spoke up. I'd never heard him talk much about God, so I was surprised to hear him become impassioned as he joined the conversation.

4. O. Hobart Mowrer, "Sin, the Lesser of Two Evils," *American Psychologist* 15 (1960): 301–4.

"We are all broken people. We are all living on grace. We all need forgiveness. I myself am a porn addict. But God understands my heart. And he knows how men are wired. He knows what I've been through and am going through. So instead of beating myself up with shame, I just trust that Jesus is my savior and my friend who understands."

As he said this, I could feel my skin begin to crawl. His little speech threatened to discount the courage I'd found in believing that God's love for me, and my love for him in return, was enough to keep me from being a slave to sin. The freedom I had felt in that moment of restoration with God was being challenged. Could I accept this "We are all sinners saved by grace" message? A message that gave me an excuse to let go of the repentance in me, to let go of the sorrow over my sin and just say, "Well, if it happens again tonight or tomorrow, I'll just ask forgiveness and accept that he understands and move on." It sounded so loving and gracious and patient. I could hear this man's reasoning unfold in my mind. *Don't be religious or self-righteous. Be humble and accept that you can never stop sinning.*

But how could I ever forget the grieving of God that I had experienced? How could I ever willingly do something that breaks God's heart, with the heart-wrenching truth that "he will understand" as my excuse? Shouldn't I be the one longing to understand his heartbreak at my sin? He has loved me so completely. I just want to love him back. I sat in silence as I wrestled with these thoughts.

Joycie's cousin broke in again. "So don't be so hard on yourself. You're only human."

This was when I excused myself to the bathroom. As I left the table, I began to see immediately how evil this guy's self-help, religious-sounding words were. He may have seriously thought he was being helpful, but he was actually giving me permission to venture off the road of repentance that I had been so certain was the right road to be on. As I realized this, I began to pray over his oh-so-reasonable invitation that was now opened up in my mind.

"Lord, let me never forget your grief. Let me never forget that your grief over my sin is because of your love for me. You desire for me to have your best in every area of my life. Help me never to forget your grief and excuse myself into willing sin. Oh, God, how disgusting to use your pain, and your suffering, and your blood as an excuse to keep on sinning. Sin is so disgusting."

I began to cry again over the gross nature of my sin in the face of his purity and goodness. I could feel his presence pushing back shame again as I locked myself in the bathroom stall, closed my eyes, and got lost in him. He began speaking to my broken heart.

No need to hide your face, my love; I want to see you. I've missed you! I love you so much! You have my grace with you and you can choose to receive it and live in it. It is not the grace to sin, but my grace is indeed the grace to overcome sin.

The relief of this promise and true comfort from the Holy Spirit washed my heart and my mind with faith and peace.

His love is so powerful. What more can I do but offer up my body and soul and freely return them to their Creator?

How can I take care of my soul?
I want to steward it well. But I need help.
Daddy, help.

Goal: Health

- Guard my heart from unhealthy relationships and situations
- Don't shy away from suffering for godly reasons in a way that produces perseverance, character, hope
- Be creative
- Listen to passions
- Seek peace
- Seek justice and purpose
- Repent quickly
- Speak life every time I am tempted with death
- Speak truth every time I am tempted to believe lies
- Find truth in the Scriptures
- Worship, soak, rest
- Resist soul clutter
- Don't fill up on junk so I will want to feast on the bread of life
- Think on things that are pure and lovely
- Flee sexual immorality

Emotional Wounds Won't Heal with Idolatry

Flash-forward. Today. Married. Covenanted.

Angry. Hurt. I ran away to breathe for a few hours.

I could feel the same old evil that parades around as "just part of life," but this demon had a slightly different name. Not sexual lust. Emotional.

My soul is tired. My soul is wounded. I notice that when I'm in this place emotionally and spiritually nothing else seems to matter.

I don't care about my hair, my clothes, whether I've bathed. I don't care whether I eat, or sometimes I don't even care if I die. There is this suspended moment of absolute delusion—that life is not worth it anymore. I lose the ability to see beauty. There is very little room to care about anything else if I don't care about myself. Even when I think I'm able to love others, when I need to be loved myself, when I need to be healed and healthy in my soul, I don't even realize the lack and deficit I'm trying to draw from.

So I ran away that night. I just needed a few hours out of the house. It was eleven p.m. when I left, and this place I found was open till one a.m. I really didn't want to go into a bar late at night without anyone with me. So I stopped and asked God, "Should I go here?" I felt a clear *yes* in my heart, so I went in with a foolish sort of fearlessness. It was a completely empty restaurant with a bar full of people on the outside patio. I sat down at an inside booth. I ordered hot tea and French silk pie. I opened my computer and wrote, freely flowing from a place of sad numbness.

I can feel a weightiness in this moment. It's weighty because I don't seem to care about anything at all. You would think that would feel light and free. But instead it weighs on me, the way being stripped of all your armor would feel in the midst of a battle. But not fearing death has certain liberty in it, too, that can lead to heroism. Insane courage.

When there is no fear of death, even for the wrong reason, we are very close to our purest purpose: to be united with God and be his immortal children, like him, perfect in love and totally devoid of fear.

How intensely sad and practically impossible for a woman with a lifetime of shame and embarrassing heartbreaks to humble herself and let herself admit all her brokenness before a God whom she must be willing to let make her new.

How empty and sad it is to have tasted a drug like emotional intimacy so powerfully.

To have that longing and aching for someone's soul that longs and aches for yours.

To connect.

To delight in.

To set ablaze.

To challenge.

And like a snowball rolling down a mountain, growing with every movement.

With every shift of the eyes when it's too close.

Too much to hold in, and you feel like crying because you feel so known, so understood, so moved and swept up.

They move you like a dance you both know.

And then, when it was all along idolatrous and leading to death, like some sweet-tasting poison, some drug that makes you feel closer to heaven than you have ever felt here on earth—I can feel the ache as I think of it.

The ache of the way it feels when the cold, bony, clawed hand grips your heart and produces blood, and you're ecstatic that you may die for your "love," your idol, your drug, because of the great delusion over your heart.

The darkness is that all you see is the love.

But this love that taunts you is a masquerade, a charade, a script that ends in torture so great there is no memory of any of the good parts you sold your soul to—anything that seemed so worth it all.

How sad to know the end is death, and long for it anyway because you feel so dead already.

How sad to also scoff at the suggestion from the enemy in these moments because you know so much better than what he is tempting you with.

It's sad to scoff because you would so much rather live dead in this life so that you can inherit eternal life. It's sad to think of having to consciously choose to live dead so that in eternity you might live fully. When there is no sin to tempt us anymore, and we have the freedom to delight in the souls of brothers and sisters without any perverted temptations or pleasures present with us here.

You can enjoy French silk pie and it has no hold on your heart.

You can talk for hours about the deep things of life and there is no rush of blood that would taunt you and accuse you of sin.

There is no sin.

There is only bliss and freedom and peace and joy and deep crying out to deep.

Daddy. I need you tonight.

Bridegroom King. I need you tonight.

Invite me to your bridal chamber and teach me what you mean when you say you cherish me. Please forgive me for ever giving my heart away. And now, how can I take it back without being accused?

And should I care that I'm accused when the accuser is a liar and just wants to kill, steal, and destroy?

Perhaps I should just, as I want to, curl up in a ball and die a little more on the outside. Run quietly and privately to some place introverted.

Is there truly an invitation from you to withdraw?

"It is not for Christians to withdraw."

But what if we are out of order? Should we wait? Should we cancel it all?

Certainly I am willing to die completely.

Then you will not believe what happened. But it is absolutely true. A strikingly handsome man walked from the outside bar into the restaurant and stood beside my table. I already knew what he wanted. I knew he was sent by the enemy of everything good in my life to test everything I had been writing about. To answer all my emptiness with solid questions. I felt this boldness that didn't fear death sweep over me. A boldness that hated Satan and was not in the least threatened by this scheme. The man sat down at my table without asking.

"Do you know why I came over here?" he asked me.

"Yes," I answered, not looking up.

"Why?"

"Because God is chasing you."

"What? I came here because you are fascinating. I don't believe in God."

"That's exactly why he is chasing you. He knows you'll say you don't believe in him, but that doesn't make him any less real. He is real and he is chasing you and that's why you are sitting here."

"I don't believe in God," he repeated. "What book is that you are reading?" He tried to change the subject. It didn't work.

"The Bible." I looked at him for the first time when I said this.

"Why do you believe in God?"

"Because I met him. On the day I planned suicide at sixteen. He rescued me from death in all kinds of ways, and he wants to rescue you."

"God doesn't want me," he boasted. He then went on to tell me how he had sexually exploited several women just last night.

"God was right there in the room with you. Do you know why? Because he loves every one of the girls that you don't care about."

"You're right," he admitted. "I don't care about them. None of them mean anything to me. They are all the same. Willing to do anything I tell them. But you. You are fascinating. You seem like you have a depth in you that I can't find in other women. I just want to talk to you because it's intriguing. There must be something you want. Something you think about. Some kind of beauty that you want. I have so much money, I could give you whatever you want."

This is when I quit looking at him and went back to looking at my computer and open Bible. I responded without looking at him.

"You don't have anything I want. But God wants you. And that's why you came over here. He wanted you to hear it and you did."

"I have to go," he said

"Of course you do," I said.

"You looked like you need something. Like you are struggling."

Then he went on to offer me drugs. I laughed.

"You are the one who needs something. You are the one struggling. And Jesus is going to follow you home, like he always does, but this time you will notice him interrupting all your plans. You won't be able to get high and you won't be able to hurt any women. The only thing you will be able to do is ask him to save you."

I shocked myself when I said all this. It sounded so impossible to know, but I was absolutely certain it was true. The strange man then introduced me to the girl who had come from the bar to leave with him. Instead of introducing myself, I told her, "God loves you more than any man ever could."

He pushed her through the restaurant door and left me alone in the booth.

I sat for a moment, realizing what had just happened.

I realized how vulnerable I was and what the offer was before me. I considered for the first time since the man appeared what was at stake in the offers I had not even flinched at. I realized the protection of Christ and the love he has for me and my family. I shuddered with thankfulness and began to type again.

Oh, Lord, your sons, your boys. Your Joshua Lewis, your Arrow David. Your Josh and your Lacey. We are yours alone; there is no life outside of you. There is no life outside of you.

I am coming to you, Jesus.

I am weary and brokenhearted.

Let me have eyes to see, Daddy, please.

Let me have ears to hear, Daddy, please.

Let me have a heart to understand.

Thank you, Jesus, for your blood. That justifies me. That invites me to the throne room of grace. Grace that empowers me to overcome sin.

Thank you that this place is open to eat so late at night when I need to get away. Thank you that there are Christmas lights. That there are Christmas songs playing. That there is French silk pie. That there is hot tea.

Thank you for a car to drive with a full tank of gas.

Thank you for money to spend.

Thank you for your yesses, over and over. You say yes.

You challenge me with your yesses.

Thank you that I am not a slave to anyone. I am a daughter of the King of heaven. He is my Father, my Defender, my Lord.

Please, Father. Please help.

Dear My Future Superman

They're gonna tell you
Men only want one thing
But I'm gonna tell you
That they don't know anything
Anything about you
But, baby, I do
Oh, I believe in you
Your breath proves God believes in you too
They're gonna tell you
You're only worth one thing
Identities in your fists or your pants
In the bank or your brains
But I'm here to tell you
Your heart's the eternal thing
What lasts is your soul
And the song that it sings

So, baby, believe me
I've seen the man you can be
Brave, powerful, beautiful soul
You're so much more than they know

They marvel at mountains
They marvel at lions and stars
They marvel at oceans
They marvel at galaxies far
But you, my child,
Hold life-giving life in your freedom
Use it for the work of God
Or you'll enslave yourself to their demons
Love doesn't trap you, my child,
Love honors freedom and choice
And you choose every day that you are given
The land of the dead or the living

You're a powerful creature, my child,
You're a powerful soul
Forever impacting God's heart
And the human race as a whole
You are a living piece of his art
And you hold a piece of his wisdom
And heaven leans in to know you
To find dormant life in you hidden

RISE &
SHINE

3/9/06 Study Title: "Subtlety, Religion, and Relationship"

Old Covenant: Can my ways ever be more righteous than what God is asking me to do? Can God use seemingly vain positions for more significant reasons?
Isaiah 7:10–17; Jeremiah 20:9; 1 Samuel 15:22; Esther 2:12–13

New Covenant: How can we confirm something we aren't sure of?
2 Corinthians 13:1

Poetry & Wisdom: Does a calling from God ever change?
Ecclesiastes 3:1–8

prayer... Father God, I belong to you. I am yours alone. So many people pull at me to be something for them, but I am yours alone. I see that I can be stubborn about things I think are right, but, Lord, make me soft toward whatever you say. Let me lay down my old ways of thinking so that I can pick up what you are trying to tell me. My heart is broken over the lack of light in the places where you have sent us before. Lord, send your light into those places. If you call us to be the light out there, then we will go. But teach us your ways and priorities and keep us from allowing ourselves to be enslaved to some situation that doesn't respect the priorities you have given us to honor in our family. And if you call us to stay home and shine our light right here in our home and community, then that would be awesome. Let us not deceive ourselves in disobedience but let love correct us. Amen.

RAK & To-Do:
- [ ] Do 20 min. stretch, cardio
- [ ] Make spinach, apple, carrot, and ginger smoothie
- [ ] Rehearse for Carson Daly Show and pack for Germany tour with Stone Sour!
- [ ] Make vegan fajitas for rehearsal
- [ ] Pick peppers out of garden, hang towels to dry on clothesline
- [ ] Give Blue Like Jazz by Donald Miller to Mom
- [ ] Take Lori out to lunch

New Song Idea: "Dear My Closest Friend"

C, A, E, F

Dear my closest friend, I'm writing because I miss you so much. At night I always cry. The stillness still reminds me of when we first fell in love, and I miss that so much. Dear my closest friend, I remember when you asked me to stay and I just walked away. I apologize. Though my letter's sent, I lost that moment, seconds at a time . . . seconds at a time . . . I wait for your answer, but I already know . . . your hand was always mine . . . dear my closest friend, I'm writing because I miss you so much.

 ## Recipe: Vegan Fajitas

INGREDIENTS:
tortillas
1 tbsp. or so coconut oil or olive oil
1 large sweet onion, diced
1 each red, yellow, and green bell pepper, thinly sliced
1 cup Portobello mushrooms, chopped
seasoning: 1 tsp. cumin, 1 tsp. salt, 2 cloves minced garlic or ½ tsp. garlic powder (or for lots of quick flavor just add taco seasoning packet)
black bean dip (equal parts black beans and salsa mixed together in a blender), guacamole or mashed avocado, chopped cilantro, and salsa

DIRECTIONS:
Preheat oven to 200°F. Wrap tortillas in tinfoil and put in oven to warm. Sauté onion in oil over medium-high heat until golden brown. Add seasoning. Add bell peppers and chopped mushrooms. Continue to sauté until peppers are tender (about 3-5 min.). To serve spoon black bean dip onto a warm tortilla as a bottom layer; next add guacamole, salsa, cilantro, and sautéed veggies, and fold over your fajita.

PM Through the Bible Reading:
Old Covenant: 2 Chronicles 20
New Covenant: 2 Corinthians 3
Poetry & Wisdom: Ecclesiastes 3

THIRST NO MORE

LIFE SONG

RETURNING MY SACRIFICES & PRIDE

Reflection

God, help me understand how obedience is better than sacrifice.

Keep Going, for Me

I knew that Miley Cyrus was in the vicinity.

I'd seen her wardrobe cases as I walked past the backstage of the indoor arena where she would perform later that evening.

What a real-life princess, I thought, marveling a bit at the endless amount of sparkly clothes she had to choose from.

My bandmates in Flyleaf and I were playing on the outside stage. The area was so packed with people that, to get to the stage, we had to be escorted by a big security guy who sporadically yelled at everyone, "Move out of the way! Artist coming through!"

This kind of thing makes me want to crawl into a hole and hide.

By the time we reached the stage, there were colored lights moving in shafts across the floor, and a gigantic Flyleaf banner made a back wall on the outdoor stage.

I could hear the guitar feedback swelling. I faced our drummer, lifted my hands, and closed my eyes to be alone with God. The sound of the voices cheering when I walked on was overwhelming.

This was our first time playing in front of a pop audience.

Our single "All Around Me" had gone on to top the pop charts, and we had only been used to playing in dirty rock clubs till now.

I heard someone say one time, "I never knew what worship was until I went to a U2 concert. The people wept, screamed, reached out with all their might, passed out from excitement, screaming their names over and over tirelessly as they genuinely worshiped the band."

Indeed, this is the way my heart feels in genuine worship of God. So many people think churches that express their love for Almighty God this way are strange, yet they don't find anything uncomfortable about people who do this at football games or concerts.

I find it strange that people can talk to Almighty God, and sing to him, without feeling like they are going to explode. But in this generation, no one thinks it strange to get caught up in pop culture hysteria.

I've wondered about this for a long time.

And on that day, I actually witnessed it. When I turned around and began to sing, I looked out at the crowd. There were people crying and screaming and reaching out with all their hearts to just touch the stage, climbing on top of each other to get closer.

A wave of nausea came over me, and I was absolutely revolted. In between the words of the song, I silently prayed and begged God to keep my heart clean, to protect me. *Help me not to throw up on them*, I also pleaded.

I was so disgusted that immediately after the show was over I walked straight to the dressing room to be alone and fell to my knees, putting my face on the floor. *Lord, please, I will give all this up for you. You are the one who brought us here. You are the one who gave us this stage. With you all things are possible. Apart from you nothing is possible. I just want to walk away from all this for you.* He whispered to my heart, *Would you keep on going for me?* This is when I first began to understand that I had an issue with pride. Not in the way most people think of pride. I was proud of my willingness to make big sacrifices, like giving up singing. God just wanted me to keep singing.

The question became: Am I willing to be considered a star? Am I willing to be a part of something that is known for idolatry, and worship God in the midst of it all, by staying when I want to leave? I was thinking, *I'll do anything for you! I'll die for you!*

And the Lord was saying to me, *I know you think that is a big deal, but the question I want to ask you is Will you* live *for me? Will you do the obvious, rational, predictable thing for me?*

Born for This

Not long after that I was on tour in Europe. There was a nice older man on the tour whom everyone called Pop. Pop was the father-in-law of one of the singers of another band. He ran some of the stage production, and everyone loved him. One day he asked me on a "Daughter and Pop" date. So he took me to a restaurant and ordered me the best thing on the menu.

"Lacey, why are you here?" he asked.

The practical answer was, "Well, the headliner invited us, and we had the dates open, so we jumped on the tour, and our record sales are up . . . blah, blah, blah."

But I could tell this wouldn't satisfy Pop. So I answered him honestly.

"You know, singing really isn't my favorite thing to do. I actually love kids. I've always wanted to provide overnight childcare in my house for parents who work at night. But I just feel like this is what I'm supposed to be doing right now."

"Well, thank God for that. Because it is what you are supposed to do. I can see that you get sad doing this. I wonder why that is. But I know you are supposed to be doing this as much as I know my own name. This is exactly where you are supposed to be and exactly what you are supposed to be doing."

"Why do you say that?" I asked, not sure if he was right or not.

"Because when you get on that stage, it's like you were born for it. It's obvious to anyone who sees you. Let me tell you something I know for sure. If you were to quit all of this today, it would just be a matter of time before it started all over and you ended up right back here again."

I smiled at his confidence in me. It was strange to hear him say these things about me, and I didn't know him all that well.

Later that day, Josh and I were walking around in a part of Germany I had never been before. We were downtown with a lot of people, and Josh had my baby Taylor acoustic guitar slung on his back.

"Let's busk!" he suggested. He pulled out the guitar to play for the passersby and sat down on the sidewalk, leaning against a wall that vaguely smelled of urine.

I smiled.

This was the kind of thing I loved. Just plopping down somewhere and playing for random people who don't know you is much more comfortable to me than hearing a crowd roar your name and then trying to remember your lyrics better than they do.

So he played a song and sang to the passersby.

Then he handed the guitar to me. I closed my eyes and started to play and sing like I was all alone. Halfway through I realized someone had stepped in front of me, because the light changed. Looking up, I saw a beautiful woman in a long trench coat watching me.

As soon as I finished the song, she leaned forward and handed me a card. "My name is Rachel. I'm here working with a record company, and I think you are fantastic. If you ever have it in mind to sing and play music professionally, please give me a call." She smiled broad and was full of vision and life. I just smiled and took her card and thanked her. I marveled at how Pop's prophetic words had just been fulfilled right in front of my eyes.

Keep singing for me, I felt God whisper.

～ℓ⌒⌒ Stewarding for the Owner of It All ⌒⌒ℓ～

Can't God demand that I <u>return</u>
My life
To him
At any moment?
"Steward,
What have you done with all I've entrusted to you?"
Distinguishing between "owner" and "steward"
Seems subtle,
But living out the difference?
The two are as different as heaven and hell.
Steward parading as owner and judge?
Lost supernatural ability to manage well.
Things start caving in.
I run myself ragged,
Lost joy,
Lost motivation.
When I pretend I am the owner,
I become deathly afraid of losing.
Owner, judge,
All is sure to fail when I deceive myself with these titles.
The steward can't make just rulings
When violating her own restrictions from God
By trying to sit in God's seat,
Because I, the steward, don't know what God the owner
    knows . . .
Not the future, as he does
Not the past, as he does
Not the intricacy of all creation, as he does
Not people's hearts and minds, as he does
Not how everything works together, as he does . . .
He is jealous over his throne in my mind
Out of protective love for me, his creation.
He knows that spot is made within me for him alone.

Anyone or anything else, especially myself, on his
    throne in my heart
Will lead to my own self-destruction.
The weight of being in this spot is too much for
    anyone but God to bear.
No one and nothing else belongs on the throne of
    God.

But when I acknowledge
Everything I have is God's,
I am free to let him be sovereign,
I am free to be empowered by his grace,
Doing what I can't do on my own.

When I acknowledge
The earth is God's planet,
I want to do all I can to care for it
And fill it with life and beauty.
When I acknowledge
Animals are all God's creatures,
Given as gifts to us,
I want to honor them
And treat them with
Compassion, respect, and diligent care.
When I acknowledge that
Humans are made in God's image,
Every human
His crowning work of art,
Each one
Worth everything to him,
When I acknowledge
God called every human
To be his sons and daughters
Through the blood
Of his only begotten Son,
Jesus,
Who died

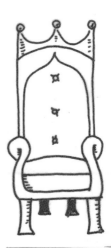

For the sins of the world
So he could redeem everyone
Who wants to be cleansed of sins and
Empowered to overcome sins by his grace
And the Holy Spirit,
Who waits for our invitation to come live inside us,
When I acknowledge
Every single human
Gets the same opportunity
To be redeemed,
Reconciled to God,
I must look on each human
With deep reverence;
I must view them
With great respect.
Because God made each
In his image,
I must view them
As God does,
As worth dying for,
Worth forgiving,
Full of potential,
Greater than
Any other precious thing
In the world.

When I acknowledge
That freedom of the will
Is a gift from God
To every person,
I will honor each person's freedom
The way God does,
Never trying to manipulate
Or control.
When I acknowledge
My husband

As one of God's sons
And realize I am
Entrusted by God
To be the closest one to his heart,
I want to love him more,
Honor him more,
I want to encourage him
Any way I can.
When I acknowledge
My children as precious
Powerful seeds
Of the future generation
Intentionally created by God,
Adored by him,
Entrusted to me,
In all their vulnerabilities,
I want to teach
Protect
Guide
Love and honor them more.
When I acknowledge that my house is a gift from
    God,
I want to care for it and share it more.
When I acknowledge that my body is a gift to me
    from God,
And that God calls my body his temple for his Holy
    Spirit,
I want to take very good care of my body.
I want to treat it kindly, and with reverence,
As if he truly made every part of me with a purpose.
When I acknowledge that my mind is a gift from
    God,
I want to renew it, guard it, grow and learn more.
When I acknowledge that God gave me a soul and a
    heart,

And that this is the place where God lives when I
   invite him to be Lord of my life,
I want to keep it clean more than any other place.
I want to worship, pray, rejoice, thank and love him
   with all my heart and soul.
I come alive in this powerful place that is my soul,
   filled with God, and this is where I truly grow.
Outwardly, I may waste away, but inwardly my
   soul can grow in glory,
If I choose to steward it well.
If I acknowledge that my life belongs to God,
I will truly live.
And when he comes for his return on the investment
   of life he made in me,
May I be able to praise God with a heart that cries,
"Thank you for your trust
Faith
Hope
And belief in me,
That you would give me life!
In all my ways,
My desire was to acknowledge you!
My hope is that because of your promise,
You were the one directing my path."
And may God's response to me be as Jesus's parable
   made me long to hear:
"Well done, good and faithful steward . . ."

HEART AT WORK

10/13/08   Study Title: "Love Is Heart Work"

Old Covenant: Why does it matter how a job gets done?
2 Samuel 6:6–7; Isaiah 1:13–14

New Covenant: Can we love with our works? Isn't belief in God enough?
Does submission begin with outward effort or with
making the heart beautiful?
Matthew 5:16; James 2:14–26; 1 Peter 3:3–7

Poetry & Wisdom: Is diligence important in a relationship?
Proverbs 31:10–12, 25–31

Prayer: Father, teach me about freedom. Sometimes I feel trapped. Show me what choices I have in front of me and give me the wisdom and courage to choose life over death in each situation. Thank you for trusting us to make choices. Thank you, Jesus, for your tears over us. Help me to always be willing to come to you and not run the other way. Holy Spirit, teach me about love. I see that all my deepest longings are really only ever satisfied in you. All else leaves me empty. How can it be that you long for us too? Is this why you weep over our unwilling hearts? Jesus, were your tears over an unrequited love? What a humble lover you must be, God, to give us choice so that we can love genuinely and freely. Love must be the most important thing of all if you would die for us to have a choice to freely love you back. You must love us so much more than we can imagine. Teach me about your love. I just want to love you back. Amen.

RAK & To-Do:
- [ ] Write with band for new album <u>Memento Mori</u>
- [ ] Make brownies for everyone
- [ ] Help finish grout on brick kitchen tiles
- [ ] Give <u>The Big Fisherman</u> by Lloyd C. Douglas to Jared
- [ ] Get guest room ready for Eric and Sarah Patrick and kids to visit
- [ ] Do 20 min. workout, run, and swim

New Song Idea:
"TREASURE"

Verse: Em, G, A · Chorus: C, D, Am

Can I tell you a story
As we dance while the sun starts to bleed
Song of songs love is calling
Daughter, wake up from your sleep (refined)

I'll be treasured over all the earth

Bearing the gift of a new heart
Em, Bm, C, D, Am, Em

Patience ablaze, I'm slowly burning

RECIPE: I LOVE JOSH FRENCH TOAST

INGREDIENTS:

4–5 slices Ezekiel 4:9
  brand cinnamon raisin
  bread (quarter slices in
  triangles or squares)
egg mixture: 2 eggs, 1 tsp.
  cinnamon, 1 tsp. vanilla,
  2 tbsp. cream (mix with
  fork until bubbly)
2 tbsp. butter or coconut oil,
  divided
1 sliced banana
1 diced apple
2 tbsp. melted peanut butter
powdered sugar

DIRECTIONS:

Dip bread squares or
triangles into egg mixture,
then fry both sides in 1 tbsp.
butter or coconut oil until
golden brown. Set aside. Put
remaining butter or coconut
oil in pan and fry apple and
banana until golden brown.
Pile this hot, delicious mess
on top of the hot French
toast. Drizzle with melted
peanut butter, then dust with
powdered sugar and serve with
a kiss.

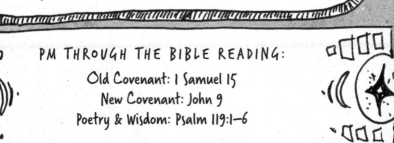

PM THROUGH THE BIBLE READING:

Old Covenant: 1 Samuel 15
New Covenant: John 9
Poetry & Wisdom: Psalm 119:1–6

HEART SONG

RETURNING MY WORKS

Reflection

Whenever I catch a glimpse of God's love for the world, I naturally desire to love God back. I want to thank him ceaselessly. It becomes a balancing act while I am in this earthly body to make sure I am not making the futile attempt to pay him for his free gift of love. These Scriptures serve as a reminder of that fact:

> We are all like one who is unclean, all our so-called righteous acts are like a menstrual rag in your sight. (Isa. 64:6 NET)
> We are saved by grace and not by works so no one can boast. (see Eph. 2:8–9)
> Faith without works is dead. (see James 2:14–26)

And when I start to love God in response to his love, I must be cautious of the tasks in life becoming more important than the relationship.

The Weight of God's Glory

When I catch the weight of God's glory, there is never enough. I want to stay in it, or near it. I never want to leave. People don't want to come back to earth after they go home to heaven, because the glory of God is the most *home* we could ever experience, endless and expansive.

It welcomes us—it's heaven's invitation to come and remain home. Heaven's glory beams as God's priceless welcome, one paid for with the most precious currency. The blood of Christ invites us in, and I never want to even come close to taking the price he paid for us for granted.

I want to stay in the glory when I touch it. The *forever* declarations pour out of my heart as I face the truth of a love I can find nowhere else. Like romance times a thousand.

Like Bono sang, "I could never take a chance, of losing love to find romance."[1]

Romance is a shadow of worship. Exclusive. Intimate. Consuming. That's why we chase after romance on earth. The shallow pool of earthly love whispers of what the deep glory ocean of worship is like with our Creator.

Worship of God extends beyond mere relationship. It is fellowship, intimacy.

I can never stay in this place long enough. I can never thank him enough. The only reason I ever stop and leave is because I hear him saying there is more work on earth to do.

But when I come back to earthly tasks, there is a looming threat at my back. Mixing up "working because I love God" with "working in order to love God" is like mixing up sex slavery with making love. He doesn't want a mere slave; he isn't demanding intimacy and service. He invites us to love him back. He wants a bride who

---

1. U2, "A Man and a Woman," *How to Dismantle an Atomic Bomb* (2004), by Adam Clayton, Dave Evans, Larry Mullen, and Paul Hewson, lyrics © Universal Music Publishing Group.

longs for intimacy and freely loves to serve. He doesn't want a servant; he wants a friend.[2]

Life in its deepest form floods my soul when I think of him. It's intoxicating. I can't help but want to run back to him in my mind every time this earthly life starts to pull me away.

When I am distracted, the ache it brings *tempts* me to worship the shadows of heaven we have on earth.

Drink. Sex. Shallow laughs.

Movies. Art. Television. Games. Books.

Food. Family.

I am painfully aware that all these things leave me unsatisfied. They are like trying to capture the fragrance of a baking cake in our mouths; playing in the aroma, we enjoy it so much, breathing it in—wondering why we are still hungry. I know it's really him I'm exploring when I encounter any goodness or joy that he has put into this earthly life. Whenever my heart burns or delights in the goodness of his earthly gifts, it's truly him alone I am longing for. I feel homesick for him all the time. It's invasive, and people around me think my desires for God are excessive. Maybe here they are.

But I have touched heaven. I have, as the Scriptures say, "tasted and seen that the Lord is good" (see Ps. 34:8).

My worship here, as I run around on earth, is just a shadow of what it is in heaven. There it is eternal.

Unless I am abiding in Christ as I work here, I am always longing to get back to him more fully. The tension pulls me always. I respond to his glory with a desire to do my earthly work well.

All the while my soul is restless.

2. John 15:14–15.

Freshly married.

My wedding day. That was the last time I had spoken with God alone.

This morning, as I stepped out of the bathroom, I found the bedroom empty. My heart fluttered and I fell to my knees on the fluffy white carpet in our new house. Josh had mentioned that he wanted to work a little on the rental apartment we were renovating.

I missed being alone with God. I cried to him. "Hi, Daddy. Thank you for a moment alone with you. Thank you for a new day. Help me know how to live this new life, Lord. How can I love you today?"

The whisper came. *Go and love Josh.*

My heart dropped. "But I want to love you. I miss you. I don't want to leave you," I pleaded.

I am always with you. Love me by going and loving my son, Josh.

"Yes, Lord," I accepted.

Josh was standing on a ladder when I entered the apartment where he was working.

His smile lit up the room when he saw me.

"Hi, beautiful! Thanks for coming to see me."

"Yeah, I was wondering if there is anything I can do to help you." I blushed.

"Well, yes! Can you start scraping that wallpaper? There is a scraper and a sponge by the stove. Just wet the paper with the sponge and scrape it off. Try not to mess up the drywall too much so we can paint it after it's done."

I kept hearing the words of my friend Victoria in my head about how her first year of marriage changed her relationship with God: All those years before I was married, I'd just read about loving people and living for God. Now I didn't have time to read or talk about it the way I used to. Being married, I actually had to live out everything I had only read about before.

What a beautiful new way to worship God.

So I went to work scraping the wallpaper like I was worshiping God by doing it. Working in God's house, for the Lord himself, getting this tacky wallpaper off his walls. Just when I was really getting the hang of it and becoming an excellent wallpaper scraper, Josh's voice cut through my concentration.

"Would you sweep this stuff up for me real quick?"

"Just a second," I heard myself say as I tried to keep focused so I could get this really big piece of ugly wallpaper off without hurting the drywall. I knew it would take me about two more minutes to finish what I was doing and I had a vague feeling that Josh would just sweep the floor himself if I didn't stop to sweep for him right then.

That's when I heard this whisper in my mind from God.

Did you come here to scrape wallpaper, or did you come here to love Josh?

I sighed out loud, feeling lovingly corrected. I put down the scraper and picked up the broom.

Again, I got to work, worshiping God by sweeping. I swept every bit of dust in every corner, and was pretty proud of my "worshipful" sweeping job. I smiled when I noticed the cloudy day outside clearing up.

Like God himself was sending the sun to shine on my sacrifice of sweeping the floors and making them sparkle.

At this moment, Josh picked up his ladder, turned it completely upside down, and dumped a huge pile of broken drywall bits that had fallen on his ladder from the hole he'd cut in the ceiling—right onto the spot I had just swept.

My mouth fell open in shock.

Just to make sure he got every tiny bit of dust and dirt off his ladder, he hit the top of the ladder against the floor, sending debris swirling into every corner of the room. That's when I felt this red-hot objection start to creep up my arms and into my face.

But before I could embrace the anger and speak up, I heard the whisper of God to my heart.

Did you come here to sweep the floor, or did you come here to love Josh?

Upon this second correction, I began to realize something. It's hard to tell the difference between working and loving sometimes. They can look exactly the same, but my heart posture is the only thing that can tell me the difference.

That's why worshiping while sitting still, reading the Bible, and singing songs to God feels like a safer way to worship. But even here, reading the Bible can turn to a quest for head knowledge instead of getting closer to God.

Prayer can turn into canned repetition or complaining and venting worries instead of having a real conversation, entrusting every anxiety to God, knowing for certain he cares. Singing songs can degenerate into trying to hit the right notes instead of a heart cry of love to the one who gave us music.

When the heart turns with a genuine love for God, the love that comes in return changes everything. God's love for us, displayed in Christ, literally shook the earth and tore down the wall between God and humanity. I believe the genuine love we share with God in return shakes heaven.

It is the way we touch God's heart.

It is the way we become conscious of eternity.

Our eternal home is utterly glorious.

～ Restless ～

Restless,
Weighty, achy, shaky,
Bubbly.

Magnetic force on my soul,
Still my body cages her in
Pressure on her wings
She's pulled hard
Against the bars
Of time and flesh.

I am drawn.
All of me
Constantly
Drawn
With the force of the current.

Somewhere
At the top of my stomach
Below my rib cage
In my throat
With rays
That shoot into
My jaw
Along
The curve of my neck
To my shoulders
A fatigue threatens me
From holding my soul and spirit in.

I am pulled.
The pulling sings to me:

"Cry. Scream.
Get Alone.
Move
With the urgent currents

In the air.
Shake
Like vocal cords
Responding to breath,
Thoughts interrupting tranquility.
Rest against the wind
Pushing you.
Let go.
Give in.
Be still.
Be taken
Into the storm
With acceptance
And peace.
This is trust.
This is your lipstick,
Your blush,
Your twirly dress,
The crown on your head.
This is reckless,
Seductive,
Alluring,
Irreverent,
Sacrilegious,
Irresponsible,
Impolite,
Unseemly.
This is
Unheard of.
This is faith."

When I become
Still,
Turning my attention
To the current,
There comes a spiritual
Emotional throbbing,

Like blood
Flowing back into a sleeping arm.
It's a painful,
Anxious moment.

How long
Will this discomfort last
Before I am back
To life,
Awake?

On the way to normalcy,
Restless,
Weighty pins and needles.
My chest feels
Strange,
Impatient:
I dream
I long
For the other side
Of this moment.
The more I focus
On the other side,
The more pain hammers my chest
With riddles of fear,
Discontent.
Something sounds
Like a distant wisdom.
It whispers:

"Embrace the present."
But it makes little sense
To the heart.

Like a song in the air,
But the volume is low.
All I want?
To hear the lyrics

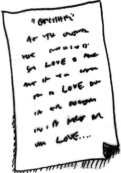

But I only get bits
Of the melody,
The snare drum,
And the word <u>love</u>
Shooting up
Like spray
From a restless ocean
I'm forbidden to enter.

But I'm the one
Who's pounded a sign
Into the defenseless,
Accepting,
Lonely palm.
"No Swimming," it reads.
I blame someone I can't see
For that dastardly sign.
But I'm the one
Who keeps it up.

There are no rules
Imposed on me
By anyone
But myself.
This my heart.
This my freedom.
This my self-imposed slavery.

I'm free
To enslave myself
If I choose.
I'm free to be free
If I choose.
I am ever free
To choose.

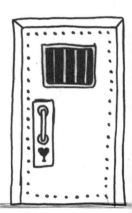

What beauty is this?
How have I been so loved?

~~~~ God's Response to Me ~~~~

Dear Lacey,

Don't get caught
Tangled in the details.
Don't get sidetracked
In the language.

Be used to my presence
As a wind moving you,
Shifting you,
Playing with your hair.
For I am
Playful and free.

I have miracles
That abide within "distractions"
Received with love.
Go ahead,
Make a plan,
Then watch me
Test your heart.
Did you come here to clean house
Or love your husband?

I have miracles
Set apart
For a life
Lived in love;
Out of that love
Flows free will loving obedience.
It's better to be a servant
In the house of God
Than to be running away from his house,
Rebellious,
Claiming it is for honesty or freedom
Or following your heart.

I would rather
Have you sort through
The nuances of transitioning
From slave to bride
In the house,
Honest with me,
Without doubting me,
Because I have miracles
Only reserved
For when an act is done with love.

This is why
Love covers
A multitude of sins:

You are not a slave,
You are my bride.

I set down one rule
To do one thing,
Right beside another rule to do the opposite.
I didn't want you to get stuck
Following rules
As you grow and mature.
I frustrated the rules on purpose.

I want you
To come to me.

I want you
To talk to me.

I want you
To have a relationship with me,
Listening for me,
Striving to look in my eyes,
To know my character
And my heart.

I want you
To know
You are not my servant
Or my slave,
You are my bride.

Obedience
Is better than sacrifice.
Sacrifice is for those without relationship,
Those slaves and servants;
But obedience?
Ah!
It's the fruit of honor,
Because it is freedom.

When I say to sacrifice
Your free will, obedience—out of your love
Transforms your response into a joy-filled privilege.
Even if you are obeying something
Once considered a sacrifice.

So,
Be a bride,
Not a slave.
This is the secret
To a life of joy.
Be a friend,
Not a servant.
Go on adventures,
Not errands.
Have me for the journey,
Not just as the destination.

Love,
Father, Son, and Holy Spirit

Study Title: "Love Will Heal the World"

OLD COVENANT: Who did God commission to rule over the earth?
  Genesis 1:28; Psalm 8; Ezekiel 16:49

NEW COVENANT: Does God care about what we do with the earth?
What is most important to God? Shouldn't we be angry and disdain
overpopulation that is "ruining" the world? Why or why not? Does Jesus
condone killing animals for food? Why isn't it a sin to eat certain foods?
  Revelation 11:17–19; 1 Peter 4:8; Acts 10:9–15; Mark 7:19

POETRY & WISDOM: Was God wise to put so many creatures on the earth?
  Psalm 104:24

...PRAYER...

Daddy, thank you for the way you have raised me. Thank you for the
way you have led me. Thank you for all you have taught me and are
teaching me now. Lord, I am overwhelmed at times with the weight I
feel to care for the world around me, but, Father, I recognize that you
are God and I am not. Please show me what I can do. I know I can't do
everything but I can do something. Please show me what that is. I know
the most important miracle I can walk in that you give me to share
is genuine love. Let your love be most important. And bless me to pay
attention when my heart burns because I know many times that it is
your heart burning within me. So if your heart is burning over these
things, show me what you would want to do through me. I love you.
Amen.

RAK & TO-DO

- [ ] Do 20 min. training, stretch, and cardio
- [ ] Figure out chords to go with kids' songs
- [ ] Make batch of vegan chili for Daniel fast
- [ ] Wash cloth diapers and hang to dry in sun
- [ ] Give Bonhoeffer by Eric Metaxas to Roman
- [ ] Buy Groundhog Day to watch with Jasmine tonight

New Song Idea: "Mama's Song"

Verse: D, G x 2, D, C, G, D • Pre-chorus: B, C, Em, G • Chorus: D, G, D, G

Verse 1: What makes you happy? What makes you smile? And when you smile please, is it for real? I know you're not one, one to pretend, even when I was a child.

Pre-chorus: You grew up too fast, and had to be brave, braver than most strong men that I've ever seen.

Chorus: Sing your song, Mama. Sing it out loud; I wanna hear your voice, it's the loveliest sound.

Mom's part— There's something I'm trying to tell you that I've tried to tell you before. And each time I confess it, it just leaves me wanting more. I think you are beautiful, and I'm proud of you. What I'm trying to say is, I love you, I love you.

RECIPE: VEGAN CHILI

INGREDIENTS:

2 tbsp. olive oil or coconut oil
2 med. onions, chopped
2-4 cloves garlic, chopped
3 stalks celery, chopped
1½ cups green bell pepper, chopped
1 tbsp. ground cumin, 2 tsp. salt,
   1 tsp. dried basil, 1 tsp. dried
   oregano, and 1 tsp. cinnamon
1 (28 oz.) can whole tomatoes, chopped,
   with liquid, and 1 (6 oz.) can
   tomato paste
2 cups canned pinto beans and 1 cup
   each canned black, kidney, and
   cannellini beans, lightly drained
1 cup cooked quinoa

DIRECTIONS:

Sauté onion in oil until beginning to brown. Add garlic, celery, peppers, and spices. Sauté 1-2 min. Add tomato paste. Sauté 1-2 more min. Add tomatoes and beans. Bring to a boil, then simmer for 20 min. or until beans are tender. Serve over quinoa or with tortilla chips. (Also delicious over plain baked sweet potato or yam.)

PM Through the Bible Reading:

Old Covenant: Joel 2
New Covenant: James 3
Poetry & Wisdom: Job 38

FLOW

RETURNING MY JUDGMENTS

Reflection

Lovers outwork workers every time.

Mike Bickle

Permission to Leave

After ten years of touring, I finally felt permission to leave music and come home to a more "conventional" type of life. When the time finally came, it was not the easy choice I thought it would be. In this season, God was showing me a new kind of pride that he wanted to die. The pride of thinking I could save people.

I didn't realize I struggled with this until all my reservations about leaving Flyleaf had to do with making sure everyone except myself was going to be all right with me leaving. The words that came over and over from God in every direction? *You are not their mother.*

When I dealt with my siblings, my heart would ache, and the Lord would speak: *You are not their mother.*

When I dealt with my friends, the same words would come: *You are not their mother.*

When I dealt with the people I worked with, it was the same. *You are not their mother.*

When I dealt with my husband: *You are not his mother.*

I began to settle into my identity as a daughter of God who was not a mother. The Lord quit saying this to me when I began to adjust my behavior and my heart so that he didn't have to correct me all the time with those same words.

I felt free and peaceful in the change. I felt new and humbled by it.

My identity as a daughter was teaching me not to worry what anyone but my heavenly Father thought of me. It also reminded me that God was a good Father to the people around me.

And I realized very clearly that I had never saved anyone from anything. God is the only one who could ever save anyone. His timing and ways are perfect, where my timing and ways were always off. What a relief to learn how to let God be God and let myself rest in being his daughter.

Then I got pregnant.

The freedom and trust I felt toward God during my pregnancy were supernatural. The first time I was alone in my house with my firstborn son, Jack the Brave, in my arms, I could feel God smiling over us.

I felt his gentle, loving whisper to my heart. *Lacey, now you are a mother.*

I cried with thankfulness.

There is a right time and a right way for every good thing. And this was the right way and the right time for me to be a mother. His ways and timing are so full of peace and order and joy.

I marveled in that moment at the strife that had been lifted off my life in the past year as I honored his discipline and quit trying to be everyone's mom. I marveled at the commission to motherhood in that moment that felt like such a peaceful gift.

Can I Have a Career and Be a Mom?

I couldn't imagine ever trying to do anything alongside being a mom. But the more I turned my heart toward being a mom and being a wife, the more my heart overflowed with writings and songs and revelations. We also had opportunities come, and my first response always seemed to be *no*.

But when I would begin to pray, the sense would come at times that we should accept certain offers. One time I went to a prayer meeting at a church, and a woman spoke to me, saying, "I don't know who you are or what you do, but I just get this sense that the Lord is saying, 'If you don't answer the call, whenever I call you, the child you are trying to protect won't have a legacy to pick up when it comes time for him to pick it up.'"

But what if I get caught up in the crazy entertainment industry cycle and never get out again? What if I neglect my family or my faith? How do I know it's safe?

Josh knew I was wrestling with all this and suggested I take some time to retreat and find some peace about it all.

One weekend I drove out to a cabin that belonged to some of our family. It was tucked away in the woods of a state park. No cell service. The only person I had to talk to was God.

The questions I wrote in my journal were How do I keep myself from making an idol of a career or ministry? How do I not lose my family in the midst of everything that could happen? How do I not lose my relationship with God?

I was listening for answers during the entire twenty-four hours I stayed in that cabin.

I read the Bible. I read some other books. I played guitar and sang. I sat still and just meditated on God's existence and worshiped. I danced around like a little kid, singing.

And I never felt like I understood the answers to my questions. Until the last hour.

I sat on the porch with my journal and a pen and wrote what came to my heart.

I was reminded of a conversation I had with my friend Christie, whose mom was a traveling pastor when Christie was growing up.

"My mom would say to me as a little girl, 'Now Jesus is calling Mommy to go and tell people about his love. If you let Mommy go with your blessing, then God has a special blessing for you. I want to give you the opportunity to bless Mommy before I go,'" Christie said. "And I would want Jesus to bless me so much that I would bless her to go. Because my mother always taught me I'm safer in the middle of a warzone obeying Jesus than I am at home in my bed disobeying him."

After I wrote this in my journal, I felt this clarity coming:

Obedience is better than sacrifice, Lacey. If I call you to go out and you stay home with your children, then you have made your home and your children an idol. This isn't good for your children when you do this. If I call you to stay home with your children and you go out to tell people about me, you have made ministry an idol. This isn't good for your children or your ministry. Stay close to me and hear my voice. I want a relationship with you that's deeper than just a line-in-the-sand rule. Walk with me and let me lead you on each adventure I have for you.

"Thank you, Lord," I breathed aloud. I was beginning to understand a little better. Then I asked him, "Is there anything else you want to say to me?"

I want you to go get your nails done, get your hair done, and buy some new dresses.

I laughed out loud as I wrote this because it seemed preposterous. I hate all these things. I hate wasting money on stuff that will grow back like nails and hair, and I hate buying clothes new when I can buy them secondhand for less—and then it's better for the world because they're recycled.

I responded, "I feel like it's you saying these things, but it really doesn't sound good to me at all. I really don't like to do those things."

What he said next has changed my perspective on life ever since.

My bride is so proud of her humility that she won't lift her head to be blessed even when I want to bless her.

I prayed, "Oh, Lord, let me never be proud of thinking I'm so humble and disobeying you in my pride."

I packed up my things and left my retreat. Once I hit a spot with cell service, my phone started lighting up. When I pulled over to get gas, I looked at my phone, and the first thing I saw was a text from Josh.

```
Baby, I want to take you to the mall to get
your nails and your hair done, and to buy you
some new dresses.
```

What?! I laughed and rolled my eyes. "Okay, God, I hear you!"

JOURNAL—05/19/12

We walked into this swanky salon full of people I had judged harshly for spending their money in a way I couldn't understand. I was escorted to a chair and began my hair transformation process.

The conversation I had with Kelton, the hairstylist, was awesome. He was brilliant and creative and God loves him so much. But after I found out that the bill was over $600, I felt sick to my stomach as I handed the receptionist my credit card. I hadn't gotten any dresses yet or gotten my nails done, and I already wanted to go home.

But I went on to the dress stores and felt that same pit in my stomach as I looked at dresses. Finally, I picked some, and we went on to the nail salon. My hands were finished and I was sitting in the massage chair getting a pedicure when I got a call from the Flyleaf manager, who was working out details about filming the last Flyleaf video shoot.

"Hi, Lacey! We decided we are going to shoot the video in Pittsburgh, so I want you to get your hair and your nails done and buy some new dresses, and we will pay for it as part of the video costs."

I sat shocked. Through tears, I responded.

"Okay. I'll send you the receipts."

I felt like God was laughing at me. He knew all along I wasn't going to have to pay for all of this, but what he wanted to point out was the fact that I had made an idol out of being "too humble" to do the kinds of things "those other" kinds of people did, like getting my nails done and hair done and buying new clothes.

He wanted to point out how my condemnation was so strong that I wouldn't even be able to hear him tell me to do something like what he was telling me to do.

I had asked God about idolatry.

And he answered me by showing me that I had made an idol out of my "humility" and was so proud of it that I would be more comfortable disobeying God and keeping a lifestyle that sacrificed nice materialistic things than I would obeying God and receiving nice things if he asked me to.

I had to return to him my sacrifices that came from lines drawn in the sand I refused to cross and unwritten laws I imposed on myself and everyone else, and learn to obey his leading in every moment, out of our relationship of trust and love.

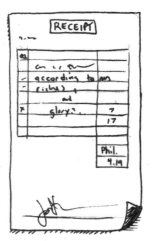

How to Eat

A year later, I made a trip to Alaska after being invited to come and share my testimony. I mentioned to an Alaskan Native—or, as they prefer to be called, Original American—that I had been a vegan for two years but had recently become a vegetarian. He chuckled and said, with a roll of his eyes, "Must be nice."

"Why do you say that?" I asked.

"You can't be a vegan here. You would die."

I sat and wondered about the winter's long months with no sunshine at all. I wondered about the struggle it took to get food into the villages where there is nothing but swampy, icy waters all around and the only way in or out is a plane.

I had struggled since I was a girl with blood sugar issues and stomach issues. In my early twenties, I tried a mostly raw food vegan diet, after many other diet changes that only made me feel worse. I was crying weekly over the frustration of never knowing what was going to trigger an episode of feeling drunk after eating something I didn't realize had sugar or carbs in it, or feeling so nauseated I couldn't function because I had eaten some kind of animal product my body wanted to reject. I prayed a lot about it, that it would go away. But I kept struggling physically, unsure how to eat.

Finally, I came across two books that spoke about the issues I was dealing with. One was called *The Maker's Diet* and the other was *The Hallelujah Diet*. Both authors had different stories about how nutrition and healthy eating had transformed their lives. I felt a jolt of hope go through me as I went to buy *The Hallelujah Diet*. Learning about health and nutrition was an amazing, practical key to entering into a new season of joy and freedom that I had never experienced in my life. So many times, when I meet people struggling with depression, fatigue, or just feeling bad all the time, I wish I could share the impact that this simple change in my life had on everything else. I started to follow the Hallelujah

Diet strictly right away. At first I felt worse. But little by little I got better, and after three weeks I felt better than ever.

I stayed on the mostly raw vegan diet for two years and was totally healed of all my symptoms. No more blood sugar issues. No more stomach issues. No more mood swings. No more chronic fatigue. I slept well. It was truly miraculous.

Then, two years in, the same symptoms returned. Little by little I started to add milk, cheese, and eggs back into my diet. And if I ate them a few times a week, I felt great. I even ate meat every now and then and felt fine with it. Along this journey, I have learned so much about my unique body and how it can heal itself if I treat it with love and care. Especially when I do it out of respect for my maker.

I remember looking at my friends, watching them eat junk food all the time. They would eat things that made me feel awful, yet they seemed to feel fine. I prayed many times for God to heal me of whatever made me so sensitive to foods, but for years I struggled. One day I was frustrated over it, and I asked God, "Why can he eat all that garbage and still be totally fine?"

He responded, *Because I made him different. And I made you different. You are more sensitive to things that he doesn't notice at all. It is the same with your spirit as it is with your body. You will feel things spiritually that others won't feel at all. You won't be able to watch certain movies, or listen to certain music, or ever hang around certain people at certain times depending on what I'm doing in your heart. But recognize this difference without judgment. Be sure to protect your heart the same way you protect your blood sugar levels and your stomach. Don't "eat" anything that isn't good for your soul, because you are wired differently. You will feel it in ways others won't. It's just the way I made you. But you must learn not to condemn the people around you because they are not like you. Love them as I have loved you.*

"Yes, Daddy. Thank you for giving me understanding. Help me."

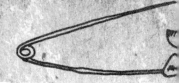

I held the phone to my ear with one hand and stirred a pot of homemade vegan chili with the other. My mom was telling me about the progress of recording her music when the subject changed to my seven-month-old, Jack. "How's he sleeping?" she wanted to know.

"Well, he is sleeping so much better now. I think the diapers we had him in were too small, so at least now he doesn't wake up crying 'cause he's wet."

"What kind of diapers are you using?" she asked.

"They're called Best Bottom, and you can adjust the size as they grow."

"I never heard of that brand."

"Well, I'm using cloth diapers."

"Why in the world would you use cloth diapers?" she asked, sounding disgusted and annoyed.

My defenses started to rise, and I got ready to argue if I needed to. So I answered, feeling overly equipped with information from several documentaries I had watched about the problem of trash in our world.

"Well, Mom, did you know that it takes five hundred years for a disposable diaper to decompose?"

There was a long pause before she mumbled a quiet, "Are you kidding me?" Then she declared, "That is so stupid. Don't you think *Jesus* can take care of the trash in the world, Lacey?!"

Immediately my mind flooded with scenes of us growing up, carrying out trash bags full of diapers and debris down three flights of stairs and across a few parking lots to the communal apartment complex dumpster.

I had images of my mom over the years, looking with adoration on each of my newborn siblings when they came home from the hospital.

I saw the times when we were all piled in the car, not sure where we were going to sleep, when we couldn't pay the rent in one place and had gotten evicted.

In a flash, I realized that the passion in my mother's voice was about her own time as a young mom.

She was defensive over her inability to add such a luxurious concern to her mind.

Her thoughts had to be fixed on things like whether she could pay for her car inspection—on top of the ticket she'd gotten for having the inspection out of date that had now turned into a warrant, the babysitter she still owed, and the rent that was past due. She had to think about where we were going to sleep next week and whether she would be able to get us to school.

I can't imagine the ridiculous notion that, in the midst of trying to survive the daily chaos of being a young, single mom with several children, she should add in to her calculations of time and money problems how many diapers the two youngest were going through, and how that impacted the amount of diapers we produced as a family, and how long that trash would stay trash, and then worry about whether we were going to significantly contribute to the destruction of the world. You can't try to save the world when you're working on keeping yourself from suffocating.

As all this ran through my mind, I stayed quiet. She was right. I was humbled by her perspective.

"Yes, Mom. Jesus can take care of the trash in the world. You are right."

I have often heard the phrase "Where there is a will, there is a way." I've found this to be very true. In my experience, the phrase is often littered with a lot of manipulation, strife, illusions of control, and bullying.

But I think what is equally true—and, in my mind, glitters with powerful purity and freedom—is "Love will make a way."

Where there is love, there is a way.

Love covers a multitude of sins.

~ℓℓℓ Judgment and Condemnation ℓℓℓ~

Judgment and condemnation,
Archenemies of the stewardess heart.
Are you doing well, steward?

Are your eyes open to what you didn't see before
When cleaning your house,
loving your spouse,
pursuing intelligence and wisdom?
Always more to do
Always more room to grow
Constantly see
places to fix.
Temptation comes:
Look at others!
What about them? They should fix that.
Judgments here.
"That's not right."
"That's not best."
Here you have moved out.
Out with the steward, in with the judge.
A steward in the judge's seat
Infects everything,
Starting at the roots.
All motivations
Are poisoned.

No pure white motivation
Only muddy gray.
The steward to judge shift
Steals your stewarding authority.
No pure black gown of authority
Only a muddy gray.

In subtle ways
Like arsenic in wine
An undetectable shift

God's gifts to steward
Become a demand for my wages.
The mentality flips.

The response to the gifts
Is no longer,
Praise God!

No.
I've worked
I've earned
It's mine.
With no God on the throne,
Why not put our wages there?
Little gold gods.
And when they don't satisfy as gods, why not
    degrade them?
Damage
Misuse
Discard
No God on the throne, it's all mine to destroy if I
    want.

But reality will prove you
Mistaken,
Fool.
Tremble at the revelation
All you are and have exists in God.
You. Are. Merely. The steward.
What have you done with your gifts?
What will you return to your maker?
I tremble
I have paraded around as owner
All before the eyes of the True Owner
Who trusted me with this life,
So fragile.
I'm returning to return it all,
Loving God back, for he is good and worth it all.

1/23/14   Study Title: "Prospering in a Natural and Supernatural World"

Old Covenant: Does God inspire artistic expression? Does God inspire celebrations or parties? Can dancing be worship? Is art valuable? Parties?
  2 Samuel 6:14; 1 Kings 6:29; 8:65

New Covenant: Did Jesus frown on extravagant, beyond-necessity acts of love?
  John 12:3–8

Poetry & Wisdom: How can we learn to be diligent? What are some benefits of diligence? Are we responsible for the earth?
  Proverbs 6:6–8; 13:4

PRAYER:

Hi, Daddy.

Thank you for a new day. You are my strength and my song. Thank you for a beautiful family. What an honor to get to serve these ones you love so much and believe in. Thank you for our home. Let it be a place of peace. Help me not to tear it down with strife or offense but to build it up with prayers of hope, faith, and forgiveness. Teach me what heaven culture is like and bring that into our house. Art, music, dancing, incense, feasting, joy, celebrations, freedom, and souls growing daily! Amen.

RAK & To-Do:

- Worship with my guitar
- Do kettlebell workout
- Make hummus, tabouleh, and guacamole for MAAP meeting tonight
- Clean off Josh's desk for him
- Give Surprised by Joy by C. S. Lewis to Dora
- Work on my book!
- Plan momma/son date with Jack the Brave

New Song Idea: "Impossible"

Verse: Em, D · Chorus: C, Em, G, D · Bridge: C, G

I can't fly, but I keep finding myself soaring high above this.
I have nothing left, but I keep on pouring out like I am endless.
Impossible . . .
I don't run too fast, but I'm looking back and miles and miles have passed.
I can barely breathe, but I'm singing out like this is nothing to me.
Impossible. . .

Chorus: Every morning I see another miracle, I can't believe I'm living the impossible. You are the sign and we are the wonder, another day of living the impossible. . .

Recipe: Tabouleh

INGREDIENTS:
1½ cups boiling water
¼ cup olive oil
¼ cup lemon juice (2 lemons)
1 tbsp. salt
1 cup bulgur wheat
1 cup celery, finely chopped
1 cup mint leaves, chopped
1 cup flat leaf parsley, chopped
1 cup cucumber, chopped
2 cups cherry tomatoes,
    quartered

DIRECTIONS:
In a large glass or metal bowl, combine boiling water, olive oil, lemon juice, and salt. Add bulgur and stir to combine. Let sit for one hour. Add cucumber, celery, mint, parsley, and tomatoes. Serve room temp or cover and keep in fridge till ready to eat. It's also good cold, straight from the fridge.

Recipe: Hummus

INGREDIENTS:
1 can (15 oz.) chickpeas
1 tsp. cumin, 2 tbsp. olive oil, 1 tbsp. lemon juice, and 1 garlic clove or 1 tsp. garlic powder
salt to taste

Blend everything in a food processor till smooth.

PM Through the Bible Reading:

Old Covenant: Jonah 4
New Covenant: Romans 14
Poetry & Wisdom: Job 39

But here in this moment I feel the worship of heaven

new blade is on further... appears slowly

repeated completely... and the beautiful staircase around

abel & disappears. Then Freedom is lit-up with the Ho...

in this moment I feel the worship of heaven while we

and the knowledge of eternity and the truth that lives there all declaring

truth about you that I have always known. You are a beautiful representative of

Christ Jesus. And I represent His Beloved. And all the songs from Heaven bring Louise

I feel my word within me. I teach them on you. That is the good ple...

SPARROW SOUL

RETURNING MY PROSPERITY

Reflection

"Josh! Josh!" my husband yelled at my oldest son above his little brother's cries. My four-year-old ignored his father and went on with his determination to hurt his little brother.

Listening to this sent an arrow into my heart. Because I know the Father does this to me. *Lacey! Lacey!* And I don't turn to hear him or stop to listen to him correct me, to rescue my loved ones from the pain I cause them, and myself, from my foolishness in my relationships and in my spirit.

Becoming a mom makes you think about the next generation with a greater sense of responsibility. And the journey of motherhood continues to teach me about the kind of love that comes from heaven.

It's a love that does not throw its weight around. It's the gentle whispers of God, calling to me. But sometimes I don't hear because of my determination to do things my way.

Lord, help me turn when you call me, especially when you are yelling above the cries of my loved ones whom I might be hurting.

Turning the Ordinary Extraordinary

God's love for us is displayed in his beauty. He has drenched the world in his beauty. Laughter is not functional. It is beautiful. Music, color, tastes, fragrances—so much beauty that is not about survival at all. It's beyond necessity. It's extravagant love from the ruler of the universe who is our heavenly Father. We become like him when we value beauty as well. And there is beauty in everything.

God's blessing to us in Christ is that we are to pray for and watch for and display God's kingdom come to earth as it is in heaven.

So what is heaven culture, and how can we create it?

Step 1: Change Your Perspective

When I came home from tour and turned my heart toward my home and my family, I found all kinds of ways to worship God in the everyday ordinary moments that turned each task into something extraordinary. When I saw all things as worship, all things became an opportunity for beauty, excellence, and love.

Making a meal out of what I had was an adventure. Cleaning the house became a quest to sprinkle order, beauty, and thoughtfulness everywhere. It made people in my home feel better in nuanced ways. The thoughtfulness of being hospitable is something that many times was just between me and God. It was a unique way of loving that no one saw and a unique opportunity to do kind things for others that were just between me and God. Like Jesus said, "When you give, don't let your left hand know what your right hand is doing" (see Matt. 6:3).

As I began to take care of my home in these ways, I found other ways to love beyond my home. Like buying food from the farmers' market to benefit the local farmers and my community. I began to recycle and made a goal to have as little trash as possible to benefit my community and the world my kids will grow up in. I tried to buy everything I could secondhand for the same reason.

The decisions I was making were being made in love. Love for God and the world he gave us, and love for my family and the world they will inherit. Making greener choices with every opportunity. I also tried to eat vegan as much as I could for the sake of my health, my family's health, and poorly treated animals. And many times I refused to buy anything that wasn't organic in order to apologize for the ways we are ruining agriculture with pesticides and commercial farming, and in an effort to help save the bees.

I purposed to teach my children about these things as well. I made an effort to make this lifestyle as easy as I could for my husband, who didn't share my conviction about all of this but looked at much of it with a suspicious notion that I had become a victim of some brainwashing propaganda.

But in my heart, I knew my decisions were made out of love. And that was most important. I knew that if I stepped into condemnation and strife to try to control or to demand others change, I would achieve nothing, because my motive would be focused on my own efforts, which can't accomplish anything outside of the love of Christ.

Many times I would see documentaries or videos that would make me feel guilty for my existence as a parasitical human and offended at the idea of having children. They just seemed full of fear and devoid of love. But the environmental problems in our world aren't a result of overpopulation.

God can feed a whole generation of people with manna from the sky and water from a rock for forty years in the desert. He can feed five thousand men with the generosity of a young boy who only had five loaves of bread and two fish. Over and over in the Scriptures, God shows us that there is always enough for people who are seeking him and that provision is never the issue.

The environmental problems we have created on the earth are the result of greed, covetousness, pride, gluttony, laziness, selfish ambition, lust, and all kinds of other sins that keep people from caring for more than just money, personal comfort, complacent convenience, selfish pleasure, and power. God doesn't honor unjust gains. He actually exposes the motives and shows how corrupt authorities in the earth lead to destruction.

But loving God and loving people will never destroy the earth or contribute to its destruction. There are times when people have to make a choice between loving one thing above another. And the priorities of love go like this: when you love God first, your marriage will flourish. When you prioritize your marriage under God, then your children will flourish in the security of your love. When your family is flourishing, you will naturally be able to grow a spiritual family. A thriving spiritual family will transform the surrounding community and the people in it. People who are transformed by the light of the Spirit will honor God's creatures, the animals entrusted to us and the environment God's given us to care for. People will always come before animals and environment. There are times when, in our corrupt world, we must choose what would seem to be a sin against one of our priorities in order to love the first things first.

But guess what the Scriptures say love does?

It covers a multitude of sins. Jesus became sin, totally died in his body, went to hell, took the keys of death from Satan, and rose from the dead. So his love has resurrection power. Love will always make a way. The Scriptures call Jesus "the Way."

How much faith do I have in God's love saving the earth? Complete faith.

How much faith do I have in my own striving to save the earth when I make my choices out of strife and fear and pride? None.

This has been my experience in every area of my life. Demanding and controlling always do the opposite of what I want to accomplish in the long run. But the grace-filled love of God in me toward others and the world around me makes miracles happen every time, especially in the long run.

Still, my own desires to be green and healthy were rooted in a true desire to love God and love the world around me, so I was full of joy and peace as I went about my efforts to do what I could.

Making homemade meals can be a lot more difficult if you don't budget your time well, which I didn't do a good job of all the time. Recycling can be like that. Going to the farmers' market can be like that. Trying not to make too much trash can be like that as well. But one of the ways I redeemed my time was to make good use of the monotony. I purposed to grow in my soul in these times.

The monotonous moments became filled with artistic expression and soul growth. I used routine chores as an opportunity to grow. I would pray, listen to worship music, or listen to teachings on something I wanted to learn about while I swept the floor or washed dishes for the thousandth time.

Laundry became a focused time to pray for each family member as I picked up their clothing. I prayed over their clothes that they would feel loved when they wore them. And, of course, the messes would get to me if I didn't remember to use these moments to draw near to God instead of break down like I have to be God all on my own.

One afternoon I was standing in the kitchen, overwhelmed by the mess. I prayed, "Holy Spirit, will you please help me clean this kitchen?" That's when the thought came, *Start with the sugar.* Then the phrase followed, *Take a lesson from the ant, you sluggard* (see Prov. 6:6–8).

As I thought about this, I realized doing one thing at a time is always doable. I put away the sugar. That wasn't so bad. Then I put away the milk. Then the olive oil.

Don't look at everything.

Look at one thing, I told myself.

Don't think about doing everything; just ask, *What one thing can I do now?*

On and on, until finally the kitchen was clean.

All of a sudden, it seemed, my house started to stay clean.

Anytime I went by something that needed to go somewhere else, I would grab it and put it where it needed to go. I attended to one task at a time like it was the only thing I had to do in the world. And that "only thing in the world" was me serving God himself.

There was joy and productivity in this like I had never known in my life.

There was no joy in the productivity. Anytime I was tempted to be excited about what I'd accomplished, I'd get behind and feel like a failure. But when I went back to finding my joy in the one loving thing I could do in the current moment, it returned.

My joy was in loving God one thing at a time, in the moment. It changed so much of the way I lived my life; all by meditating on the verse, "Take a lesson from the ant, you sluggard," and envisioning an ant carrying one grain of dirt at a time and building a grand ant farm by doing it. Ever since then I have wanted an ant farm. Maybe someday.

Step 2: Understand a Love beyond Necessity

One day I was walking down the steps in our house and I could feel depression looming like I hadn't felt in so long. It was circling my head and getting into my ears and eyes. I could feel it pulling down the corners of my mouth, and I cried out to God, "Help! Please."

The whisper came. *You are in strife and you are operating in Adam's curse. Come into the Sabbath of Christ. My love is beyond necessity. Live here where I am free to love you extravagantly and you are free to love extravagantly like me.*

Okay, I thought. *How can I live beyond necessity while I walk down these steps?*

Sing.

I began to sing, "I'm on my way down the steps to tell my man to call his dad. I answered his phone 'cause he left it alone and I wanted to help him out."

The song didn't make me feel better. I felt nothing. But I kept singing. Making up melody and singing stupid words.

As I passed by my children, I wondered, *How can I live beyond necessity as I walk past my children? Kiss them,* I thought. So I walked over to them. "I love you," I told them and kissed each of them.

How can I live beyond necessity as I walk down the hall?

Keep singing.

I found Josh.

How can I live beyond necessity as I tell Josh to call his dad?

I can thank him for something. I can kiss him. So I thanked him for something, and when I went to kiss him, he held on to my arm and kissed me again.

I felt the rush of love he was giving shoot me in my soul. I felt a choice looming above my head, caught up in the cloud of depression above me. The choice was *Receive his love, or reject it, because he doesn't care to know what you are going through inside and you can accuse him instead.*

The beyond-necessity choice is to receive his love.

So I smiled.

I softened.

He went back to work.

I went back to the living room.

Beyond necessity in the living room? I lit my favorite candles, still feeling sad. I put on my favorite jazz song. I walked outside and began to list anything that came to mind with a thank-you in front of it.

Thank you for music.

Thank you for the sunset.

Thank you for children.

Thank you for candles.

Thank you for marriage.

Thank you for a home.

Thank you for your love.

Let me feel it. And all of a sudden I was in a conversation with God and my heart was lifting.

Step 3: Let Intimacy Fuel Your Love

We love for Christ's sake. He washed Judas's feet. How much more are we to love and serve and wash the feet of those God has put around us? If loving others is ever a drain and a chore and a grumbling feeling of slavery, you're doing it wrong.

After he washed the disciples' feet, Jesus said, "A new command I give you: Love one another. As I have loved you, so you must love one another. By this everyone will know that you are my disciples, if you love one another" (John 13:34–35).

Later on, after Jesus returned to heaven, the apostle Paul reminded the Christians in Rome that loving God looks like sacrifice: "Offer your bodies as a living sacrifice, holy and pleasing to God—this is your true and proper worship" (Rom. 12:1).

The love Jesus showed through the sacrifice he gave reveals a heavenly kind of love, at once strong and vulnerable. A love so intimate, I often blush describing it.

Learning Love through Worship

There are seasons in which our worship style will shift. As a baby Christian, I stayed at my heavenly Father's chest. He held me, comforted me when I cried, and obliged my silly requests, so I would know that he hears.

I learned that he's faithful.

I learned that he's extravagantly loving.

He is never annoyed or exhausted with me.

He is purposeful and intentional in letting me know that he is trustworthy.

He was kind enough to build trust in me, patiently, as I fumbled through with honesty and questions.

Finally, after enough time, he called me to walk on my own. I now know more about his character. I know his voice better. I know his heart and love for me more than ever. I know him a little more, and he can set me down.

If I cry when he sets me down, he waits for me to realize that I'm still okay and that he hasn't left me. When I realize that he still loves me, I can relax. Then I can enjoy his delight in me as I start to walk on my own.

When I worship God in this season, I try to go to him one-on-one. I try to find his joy when I pray. I try to find his joy over me when I read the Scriptures. I wait for his joy to flood my heart when I listen to worship music. My brain just spins in all of these things. I feel there is only information going in. I don't feel the intimate connection with God that empowers me as I used to.

It's his joy over me that pours heat into my soul and makes me strong and brave and able to do what I couldn't before. But I'm still searching for it in this season. So I read other books by Christian authors, and some of their words are life-changing, powerful, leading to repentance. But still, I feel far away from his intimate joy over me, the difference as gaping as the gap between going to school and making love.

In this faraway place, when I go to do what I think might make God happy, like I do in many areas of my life, I feel like a slave—a willing slave, but still a slave.

In the midst of my willing slavery, a phrase lights upon my mind. This is how God's voice has to come to me over the years, so I pause. *Love Josh.*

"Yes, Lord." I answer as usual. Willing Slave's favorite line is, "Yes, Lord."

But when I go to obey the command to love Josh, something happens.

I feel the Spirit of God moving through me. The joy of the Lord over me takes my breath away. All it takes is me looking at my husband with the intention of actively love-as-a-verb loving him, and I feel like weeping or dancing and I am rushed with energy. I don't care if I die doing it, there is so much Holy Spirit, so much eternal-minded, purposeful worship and love of God in my heart. I have no expectation of the results of my love; my service is not slave work to be resented or to keep myself from getting a beating, or to buy some credit or love in return.

I am high on the act and intention of loving Josh out of worship to God. If I purpose to love him however the Lord would show me to love him, I will do it with joy, worship of God, excitement, energy, purpose, creativity, and pure love.

Much like when I volunteered for Samaritan's Purse in Alaska. My heart was so excited to serve! And love! I was not paid in anything except the rush of the worship experience with God. I was living in worship. The moment my heart turned toward the people for approval or love in return, it became business and idolatry. The moment I made it about religious piety, it became stiff-necked, nose-up pride; the moment I made it about martyrdom, trying to pay back God, earning his love and forgiveness, or trying to make myself in some way worth it to him, it was religious pride, performance, fake smiles, acting the role of "God's-bought-my-life-with-the-blood-of-Christ" slavery.

But when I did it in worship—a free offering of my body with joy, like dancing, like a jumping up and down at Christmas that can't be helped—and thought of it as loving God and pleasing him out of pure love for him, affection for him, desire for him, worship of him, I could almost instantly feel his pleasure, and this was my pleasure.

So intimate, like the best kind of lovemaking.

Your pleasure is to see your loved one pleased.

Their pleasure is to see you pleased, and you are free to be pleased and rejoice and laugh and feel free and yourself, and to want more because it is so pleasing to your lover.

This was worship, this was intimacy, this was love. Love for God in loving others. Not so they will love you or so that God will love you, but because God loves you; it's your love-him-back overflow response.

And because you want to love God, you set your heart solely on serving him. And as he sends you to love others, you feel his deep pleasure, even if the others you are sent to love reject you. You aren't there for them.

You are there because you are worshiping God. You could be walking before a firing squad with a smile because of pure love, and having felt his pleasure, there is no guilt, no compulsion, no religiousness, no trying to pay for your sins or earn your forgiveness, no trying to be a great-pious-pompous-better-than-the-average-joe-proud-of-your-humility martyr.

It's not because you want to be somebody.

It's because you love God and you don't love anything more.

Is it easy when you feel like garbage? When your hormones are out of balance? When you are physically ill or tired or hungry? No.

It is in these moments that we may choose right behavior out of the hindsight of our covenant love. These are the moments for which we make covenants. Because, like Job's testing, we make grand speeches when we feel well, and then the devil proves if we are a liar.

Are we a truth-teller or a liar? We don't know until we're tested.

But once the test comes, and we live in that moment—in that season of testing, of choosing truth despite our feelings—it is then that we stand in the beauty of a covenant moment. It is then that we meditate on what God has done all along the way to show that he is and always will be worth it, that all the suffering will produce glory and hope.

Like it always has.

Love Note from God

Dear Lacey,

You are my princess. Carry yourself like you are who you are.

When you get out of bed, make it look nice like you are thankful for the covers and pillows and the rest it gives.

When you take a shower, remember it is me who cleans your soul.

When you put on lotion and perfume, remember that I gave you flowers because they are beautiful and that is what my love is like. So make yourself beautiful too.

Your husband loves your hair, so take care of that too. It will be an act of love to him when you do.

When you eat, eat healthy like you care about the body I've given you. And enjoy it like you know that I love you.

And when you use things, try to leave them better than they were before you arrived. This is the way heaven impacts earth. So be a citizen of heaven on earth.

Be kind to your husband and children, and know that I am loving them through you.

Take time to exercise. And when you do, spend time with me. It's good for your spirit, mind, and body.

Clean your car like it is a chariot from heaven. This will be a reminder to you to be thankful, for it is a gift from me. Make your home a place your family loves to be and fill it with beauty and order. This is heaven culture.

Dance.

Laugh.

Sing.

Paint.

Even if you feel you don't know how and aren't good at it.

Draw.

Cook.

Be silly.

Write poetry and stories and funny songs. But above everything I've said here, the heavenliest thing you can do is the most important action: you must *love.*

Remember, nothing you could ever do could make me love you any more or any less.

—*Papa*

1/20/15 Study Title: "Eat with Love"

Old Covenant: Are animals valuable to God?
  Numbers 22:21; 2 Samuel 12:1–6

New Covenant: Can a Christian survive being poisoned? Should we test God? How do we impact creation?
  Mark 16:17–18; Acts 28:3–6; Luke 4:9–12

Poetry & Wisdom: Can we learn about God's love in caring for animals?
  Psalm 23

◇—◇—◇—◇—◇—◇—◇—◇—◇—◇—◇—◇—◇—◇—

Prayer:

Father,

you're so beautiful. You have given us so many gifts. Thank you for creating a world for us to live in with such thoughtfulness and love. Thank you for giving us life to steward. Your trust in us is astounding. Let me trust people with the hope and faith in them that you have. Let me see through your eyes.

   I long to.

Amen.

◇—◇—◇—◇—◇—◇—◇—◇—◇—◇—◇—◇—

RAK & To-Do:
◯ Record for new album
◯ Do 20 min. run, 20 min. kettlebell swings
◯ Make brownies for studio
◯ Give The Neverending Story to Josh
◯ Help clean out Mom's fridge

New Song Idea: "Feels Like Forever"

Verse: Em, D, C, D, Em · Pre-chorus: C, D · Chorus: C, D, Em, G

Verse:

My hands are burning again tonight
My heart's awake but I don't feel right
Oh, I can feel the heat rise
If I could stand up and face this light
Tearing apart my old disguise
But I can't open my eyes, still I see you

Chorus:

My mouth is cold, my body whole
I may explode but you feel like forever
And I'm temporal, your temple
I may explode but you feel like forever
I'm falling over and into you
I am consumed and you feel like forever

RECITE: BROWNIES

INGREDIENTS:

1 lb. butter (4 sticks)
6 oz. unsweetened chocolate
1 lb. (16 oz.) semisweet
  chocolate chips
6 extra large eggs
3 tbsp. instant coffee
3 tbsp. pure vanilla
2 cups sugar
1¼ cups all-purpose flour,
  divided
1 tbsp. baking powder
1 tsp. salt
12 oz. chocolate chips
1 cup smooth peanut butter

DIRECTIONS:

Preheat oven to 350°F. Butter and flour a 12 x 18 x 1½ inch baking sheet. Melt butter, unsweetened chocolate, and 1 lb. semisweet chocolate chips together in a large glass bowl. Let mixture cool a bit. In a medium bowl, mix eggs, instant coffee, vanilla, and sugar till frothy. Pour this egg mixture into your slightly cooled chocolate mixture. In a separate bowl, sift together 1 cup flour, baking powder, and salt. Slowly stir into the chocolate mixture.

In a small bowl, toss remaining ¼ cup flour with 12 oz. chocolate chips. Gently fold this into the batter. Pour batter into prepared pan. Spoon peanut butter on top and swirl with a butter knife. Bake 25 min.

PM THROUGH THE BIBLE READING:

Old Covenant: Job 39
New Covenant: Romans 14; 1 Timothy 4
Poetry & Wisdom: Psalm 8

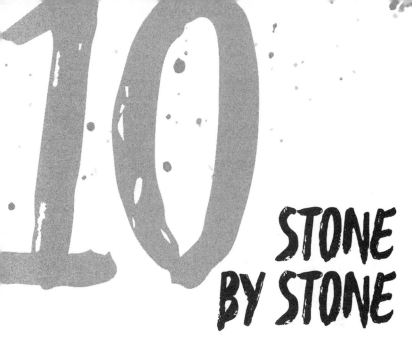

STONE BY STONE

RETURNING MY HOSPITALITY & INTENTIONS

Reflection

"Thank you, God, for this cow that gave its life so I could eat a delicious hamburger for dinner, and I pray that the cow would be at my house when I get to heaven one day so I can thank him myself." My five-year-old lifted his head from his prayer and said, with a big smile, "Amen!"

I love being still enough to appreciate what is going on in my kids' hearts. Discovering what they are learning and how they are growing into awareness and gratitude is a beautiful thing to witness. Many times life can get so busy that we don't know how to be intentional with the "little" choices. But I have learned that not many of our choices are "little" ones after all. We all need to give and receive the hospitality of intention—not just making choices arbitrarily but with awareness and purpose. Hospitality comes from the root word *hospital*, a place of healing, where teams work inten-

tionally to make people better and well. We can all grow into this
if we pay attention.

God Builds Love into Me, Stone by Stone

I saw a wall of stones as I was praying for Josh and the kids and
our ministry. I was praying for order and wondering how to steward
everything we had going on.

I realized the other day how little I look into my children's
eyes in order to understand them better. I'm always telling them
to look into my eyes to be sure they understand me, but I hardly
look into their eyes for that purpose. When I do, I get butterflies
in my chest with wonder. I can sense their freedom and purity
and total rest in me as their mother. I see a love in them that is
earthshakingly genuine.

It transforms me a little.

And my honor and love for them make me tremble in those
moments. I realize they are truly divine gifts from heaven to the
earth and I am responsible for stewarding these little gifts of mine
and my home and the world around them.

I'm responsible for preserving that purity and being transformed
by it to some degree. To look at them and be in wonder over them
is to enjoy them for the gifts they are. But I notice that if I look at
them only to manage them, then my joy gets stolen and stunted and
turns into mere fleeting happiness over my own management skills.

If I throw a party with expectations, without letting the celebration move me into what it really wants to become, letting
myself be surprised at how it unfolds and appreciating the way
things change, then my celebratory heart is changed to a stressed,
anxious, disappointed, or angry one.

The joy is stolen.

The party was meant to be a gathering with friends and family
and I should be happy and rejoice. Instead, at times my happiness
is stolen by expectations I can't make happen organically. I can run

myself ragged and feel like a slave to the people I'm supposed to be loving at the party I'm supposed to be enjoying.

But *presence*, coupled with gratitude, honor, genuineness, honesty, and love everywhere, will keep my enjoyment on and my party free and fun. And these are all stones in the wall God wants to build into our foundation.

Building Love, Stone by Stone

Presence—being fully present.

Gratitude—never taking things for granted.

Honor—acknowledging all creation is God's artwork and is able to grow my soul in all kinds of ways if I look for its great value and let it.

Genuineness—never being pulled into politics, or people pleasing, or flattery, or religious obligation. Never violating my own will or allowing myself to be manipulated.

Honesty—never being deceitful with myself or anyone else.

Love—always being motivated by love as defined in Scriptures.

How does love relate to hospitality? How does it guide my choices?

Love extends far beyond the functional part of mere hospitality. Meeting needs is important for survival, but the struggle to survive is a struggle that has come to us through the curse of Adam. The change that comes to the world through Christ is that he removes the curse of Adam when we put our hope in him.

A close friend of mine told me during a deep conversation about faith that he believes eating meat is immoral. "But what if it's all you had to live on?" I asked him. His answer was very firm and forceful, but I still wonder if it could be true in reality: "I would die." He stared into my eyes with such conviction that it made me sad to think of that ever happening. It made me sad to think that he didn't consider his life more important than an animal's. That perhaps his philosophy didn't acknowledge the honor that animals may have been given by God (and may even be happy to give if they were to know what they were doing) to give their lives for the people who are nourished by them. But I do respect and appreciate so much the idea of being intentional with food choices. Not complacent. Not turning a blind eye to the process and the evils we may be ignorant of in the way we eat and the way we live. We should know and care about what we spend our money on and be intentional to make choices of love the best we can.

No Curse on Food

Jesus was resurrected from the dead. He overcame the grave.

When Jesus died and rose from the dead, he made all animals clean, because he overthrew the old order of what sustained life and what brought death.

It's my righteousness that keeps me healthy in body, soul, and spirit. And what I eat or don't eat doesn't make me righteous. It's Christ who makes me righteous.

Every animal that is used for food, because of the salvation that came to the world through Christ's death, is now a symbol of what Christ has done for us, if we will recognize it. It is a moment to give thanks.

How can any food be unhealthy if the Holy Spirit of God living inside us, who raised Christ from the dead, is who gives life to our mortal bodies? Doesn't that make all foods fine to eat, when we give thanks for them? Every animal that died, whether it was brutally killed as Christ was brutally killed or humanely treated and then killed, preaches the gospel to us when we thank God for the life of the animal given to us for food and ask God to bless it and remind us of our salvation through Christ.

Bread is supposed to remind us of Christ's death for us. How easy is it for us to remember Christ when eating an innocent animal that was once alive and died for our nourishment?

So must I demand that all people not eat meat or eat only humanely treated meat? No, but if God tells *me* that I must eat this way, then yes, *I* must. If it burns in *your* heart to refrain from eating meat for some reason, then yes, perhaps this is God giving *you* a beautiful part of his heart to shine in the world. One that preaches a unique heavenly wisdom about how in the kingdom of heaven there is no more death. And the only death we need to give us life ever again is the death of Christ, and that has already been accomplished for us.

This burning comes into my heart so often. During a time when I had just sorted out my health issues by changing my diet, God put me in a situation where this was tested. It's like he was asking me, *Do you trust in food, or do you trust in me?*

While recording Flyleaf's first album, I stayed in Los Angeles for two months. In California, they make it so easy to eat vegan, and I felt

so great. Usually, if I had meat or animal products, or white flour or processed sugars, I felt terrible right away. But when I got home from California, I stayed a couple days with my grandmother. Someone had mentioned to her that I was a vegan now. She joked about how "vegan" sounded like some kind of alien life form. But out of love for me, without me asking her to, she wanted to surprise me by accommodating me as best as she knew how. Everything she offered was full of cheese, dairy, processed sugars, and white flour, but she had spent money she didn't really have to spend on these special meals that she fixed me. I didn't dare refuse the food. But guess what? God blessed me as I thanked him and ate, and I never felt bad the entire trip. I ate in love. I ate in faith. And God honored her love for me and my love and respect for her in return.

So long as I am not being unloving to someone by my refusal, I will, as often as I can, choose not to eat meat, because doing so makes me feel better and because I don't want to be a part of death. But this is not a superior moral place; it's just my particular feeling. Someone else may feel close to God as they thank him and eat meat. And that is accepted by God. So who am I to judge his child or not accept him? No one. In the Scriptures, 1 Timothy 4 warns us against this kind of forbidding and judging, saying that in the last days it will be a demonic strategy to carry us away from our faith in God.

Is it okay to mistreat animals? No. There is a story in the Scriptures about a man who was abusing his donkey, and an angel appeared and told the man, "If the donkey hadn't seen me and stopped you from crossing where I am, then I would have killed you and spared the donkey" (see Num. 22:33).

In this moment of animal abuse, the angel of God declared the animal more worthy of life than its abuser! God also considered how many animals were in Nineveh when he explained to Jonah why he didn't want to destroy the city without giving them a chance to repent (see Jon. 4:11). Also in the Scriptures, King David said a

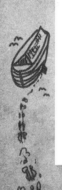

man deserved to die for stealing someone's only beloved sheep and slaughtering it to give to his visitors for dinner (see 2 Sam. 12:5–6).

God rescued all the animal species on the ark for a reason. God talks many times in the Scriptures about how much he considers animals and how he has put them in our care as gifts to us from him. There are laws against mistreating animals both in Scripture and in our country for a good reason.

But the Scriptures also say that, in general, an animal's life and a human life are not on the same level as far as worth and value to God. We are God's children; animals aren't made in his image or considered his children. Jesus said, "You are worth more than many sparrows," and you are worth "much more than a sheep." He also said it is not right to "take the children's bread and give it to their dogs" (see Matt. 10:31; 12:12; 15:26).

The problem is that because of the way our world is, there is no way for some people to even consider not eating meat, or eating only meat treated humanely, because of their circumstances. People are worth feeding, and there is always enough if we are thankful for what we have and eat what we are given out of love.

But there are those who have the luxury of choosing whether or not to eat meat or only humanely treated meat, and for them it is good when they make choices to encourage kindness, good stewardship, and respect of animals as God's gift to us. Some are even called to try to make great changes in the way the world is so that we can all more easily be kind, no matter what our situation is.

And what of people who eat poorly for their health? Is it okay to eat any way we like?

Well, if Jesus rose from the dead and he gives life to our bodies, then it isn't food that gives us life. It is the Holy Spirit. But for some reason food is a central part of family time and celebrations in the Scriptures. God has given us so many ways to stay healthy by how we eat, including natural cures to common ailments. It would help so

much, in a natural way, for us to pay attention to what we eat. But if we don't have that luxury, which many people don't, then we can be sure it is Christ who gives us life and not food. When Jesus was tempted in the wilderness by Satan, the devil said to him, "If you are the Son of God, turn this stone into bread." Jesus was fasting, so he refused, and he reminded the devil of the Scripture that says, "We don't live by bread alone, but by every word that comes from the mouth of God" (see Matt. 4:3–4).

But we must be careful not to take a promise like the one in Scripture that says, "You can drink poison and it won't kill you, or take up serpents and they won't harm you" (see Mark 16:18), and think it means that we have a free pass to act foolish or any way we want.

Jesus showed this when Satan tempted him to jump off a building. "If you are the Son of God, jump down from here, for the Scriptures say that he won't let your foot dash against the stones."

And the answer of the Lord was, "It is also written, you shall not put the Lord your God to the test" (see Matt. 4:6–7).

But no matter what our situation, or our decisions about what we eat, it is the Spirit of God who gives us true life. And in the end, one person who eats very healthily could have health problems and the one who eats very poorly could be totally healthy. The most important thing is that we do what we know is good for each of us and that our decisions are made in love for God and for others.

~˜˜˜ Aching Nothing ˜˜˜~

No running to food today
I'm fasting.
No running to movies or theatre
There aren't any on.
No running to small talk
No one to talk with.
No running to business or work
No way to work.
No running to friends or family
No friends or family around.
No running to my role as a wife for identity or
    purpose
No husband to care.
No running to my role as a mom
The kids are safe and sleeping.
No running to chores
They are all done.
And I feel so empty I could implode.
Like an itch I have to scratch
A sore muscle I must rub
A wound I have to cover
My soul wants to be turned inside out so I can
    massage the ache that is so persistent and
    distracting.
My soul is being pulled into the nothing, a black
    hole.
What does the nothing look like?
It looks like being blind.[1]
Like I can smell an orange but can't taste it or see
    its color.
Like I can feel the warmth of the fire but can't see it
    light up the darkness.
Oh, persistent ache

---

1. Michael Ende, *The Neverending Story*, trans. Ralph Manheim (New York: Puffin Books, 1993).

Achy discipline of God my Father who
Backs me into corners and lets me get caught in my
    own pursuit of
False, dead-end idols.
Like Edwin Abbot's <u>Flatland</u> he says, "You must
    come up."
But I'm only two-dimensional and want with all my
    heart to come "up"
But instead all I do is go forward.
I don't know how to explore height.
I get caught in the duties in front of me and never
    learn to rise
Because I keep moving forward.
Make me still, God, so I might rise.
Help me find the place to stop.

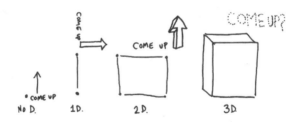

INTERLUDE

AERIAL VIEW (RETURNING MY LOVE)

Where is my phone? Lost again; for the millionth time. That means I don't know what time it is. I don't even know what day it is. All I know is the sun is up and my kids are still asleep. So I'm writing. This is the first time I've written in this brand-new MacBook in seven months. For two of those months, I wasn't sure where it was.

As I typed that last sentence, I went to scratch my head, and the last of my extensions (or as my beautiful black friend Jasmine, who has gorgeous all-natural hair, calls it, my "white weave") fell out. I had them put in a month ago, after my hair burned off from bleaching it at a nice salon that I went to so I could be sure my hair wouldn't get burned off by bleach.

I did happen to get all the laundry done yesterday for the first time in about three weeks. But since it didn't get done till the evening, my two boys were running around outside all day yesterday sweating profusely in winter clothes while it's only just now nearing the end of summer.

I washed the dishes yesterday for the first time in three weeks as well. So my sister went around the house placing cups of apple cider vinegar everywhere to collect all the fruit flies.

For the past three weeks, I have eaten more sweets, meat, cheese, carbs, and fried stuff than I have in months. I had a corndog and frozen meatballs for dinner yesterday, as did my two sons. I have mostly been on the couch or in my bed for these past three days as well and haven't exercised at all.

After seeing his father build a house for his family, my husband has had a dream in his heart since he was a little boy to build a house for his family. And after eight years of marriage, saving up money, and moving in and out of relatives' houses and rentals, he is almost finished building a place for us here in Pennsylvania. I must add here that we are currently in marriage counseling because we are trying to love each other through all of this.

Most days we are "squatting" on our own property because we don't have an occupancy permit yet. But when we are working late nights and early mornings on the house, it's best to let the kids sleep here.

So I have assembled two big pallets, or makeshift beds, on the particle-board floor in their future bedroom that consist of pretty much every blanket we own piled on top of each other to make them as soft as possible so they sleep through the night and don't wake up grouchy.

Let me add here that I'm currently in the middle of reading *How to Set Limits for Your Strong-Willed Child*. I have two of what the book describes as strong-willed children. Meaning that long after we have grown tired of disciplining, my children are not yet tired of testing whether we really mean what we say.

Some of our belongings are here in the new house, where we are squatting, some of them are at my mother-in-law's, where we are technically supposed to be living, some of them are in our shuttle bus that Josh turned into our tour bus about seven months ago, and the rest of our belongings are spread out between three different storage places.

I have been to Walmart more times in the past seven months than I have in my whole life. I haven't recycled in those seven months and probably produced more trash during this time than I have in several years.

As odd as it may sound, that is the first sentence I've written that makes me tear up.

The last time I bought groceries to make a home-cooked meal was . . . I can't remember. The last time I cleaned my car was probably around the same time.

My armpits smell like there are gorillas somewhere in the vicinity and I need a shower. But I'm not going to take one. Because when a moment of revelation happens, stewarding the revelation is more important than bathing.

This is how our souls grow.

And the revelation I have come to this morning, as I reflect on all of this, is that although it looks like everything is chaos, I can say with confidence that the state of our lives is a direct result of choosing to love. I'm resisting the urge to explain why this is true, because part of my soul-growing journey is learning to not start defensive speeches about why I have good reasons for all the questionable-looking things in my life. God's teaching me to stay humble and not try to explain every detail of my reasoning to people who probably aren't even judging me. He can defend me if he wants, and if not, then I'm learning to rejoice in that. But as I examine my heart, I find a delightfully stabilizing peace in realizing that this craziness we are walking in is the aftermath of crazy love choices.

In the prelude, I expressed my desire to write to you about taking care of, or stewarding, your gifts.

And the greatest gift you can give the world is your love. Love brings life everywhere it goes. I must confess, I used to be one of those people who condemned and judged people based on what their circumstances looked like. But I have learned the hard way to stop doing that. And when I feel like all the judgment and condemnation has been beaten out of me, another situation comes around the corner, and I find a new log sticking out of my own eye.

Jesus said, "How can you take the speck out of your brother's eye when you have a log in your own eye? First take the log out of your own eye and then you will see clearly to take the speck out of your brother's eye" (see Matt. 7:3–5).

We can help people find clarity to certain degrees, but not until we have stopped condemning and judging and showing prejudice. And when we have been thoroughly humbled and humiliated and freed from thinking we know everything, then we can finally help bring some clarity to others. I like to let God be the judge. And then I can be his witness. Just tell what I've seen. Easy!

Choosing love is the only reason I can find for how, in the past five years, I've managed to keep two children alive and growing in their hearts, minds, bodies, and souls.

Choosing love grows my marriage in these same areas.

Choosing love is why we released a full-length album, and I believe why it is selling so well. My husband and I chose to love God by obeying his nudges to our hearts to write music and share it, even when it was inconvenient and expensive and had no guarantees of success or financial return. We chose to love the fans by responding to the thousands of emails I received asking for new music and writing music for them that addressed many of the things they were struggling with and wrote to me about. We chose to love our kids by teaching them that instead of hiding from the dark in the world, we face it and shine our light into it and bring the love for Christ into places where people don't know that they are loved.

Choosing love is why I released my first book, *The Reason*, about overcoming suicide. I chose to love the fans by answering so many of their questions about depression, suicide, and my faith in Christ. I chose to love my husband by honoring his suggestion that I should write a book.

Choosing love is why I released my second book, *The Mystery*, about finding emotional purity and health in my romantic life. I chose to love God by honoring the urgency he put in my heart to share how he defeated the enemy in my life in all these areas. I chose to love the fans by writing *The Mystery* in response to the many emails I received from people in abusive relationships or affairs, or who just wanted to know about healthy ways of dating.

Choosing love is why I've gone on four national tours and taken numerous speaking appearances. Each time an opportunity arises, my husband and I pray and seek to obey the leading of God on each invitation.

Choosing love is why I believe these things were accomplished in the past five years.

Choosing love is why I am at home right now until next year. Loving my family by acknowledging that we need a break and we need to build ourselves up relationally, spiritually, and emotionally. Loving God by obeying this sense that he is calling us to be home for a season.

Choosing love is why I'm writing this book. I long to reach out to the people who long to know more about answering their calling and loving God back and stewarding his gifts with joy. I long to show people that the best way to spend your life is to spend your life choosing love.

Because when we choose love, the ripple that comes from that choice is life. Life and more life. It turns into a wave of life.

And when there is a great wave about to crash as a result of all your choices to love, it often looks like everything is lacking. The shoreline pulls in. The bigger the wave, the farther the water goes out.

In those moments, people can look around and call it a desert. And if you don't condemn yourself for what looks like a desert around you, there are certainly those who will.

And my testimony is just what I have seen personally, in my own experience. It might not relate to everyone, but it also might help some stand up with more confidence in their purpose and coast with more freedom and peace into their destinies.

So, as I said earlier, it is out of choosing to love that I write this in the middle of all that is going on around me.

Choosing to love God by giving my testimony about how his ways are miraculous and beautiful.

Choosing to love my husband by fulfilling the commitments we made to our publisher, which is always important to him.

Choosing to love my kids by teaching them what obedience and commitment look like as I write this.

And choosing to love you by sharing some of my revelations about stewardship so I might help you to know that you are loved and give you courage to choose to love when it's difficult.

I don't remember asking to be born.

None of us do.

But we have been given this gift of life by our powerful, beautiful Almighty God. Figuring out how to steward this gift of life I have been given is one of the greatest adventures I have ever been on. I'm still learning about it every day.

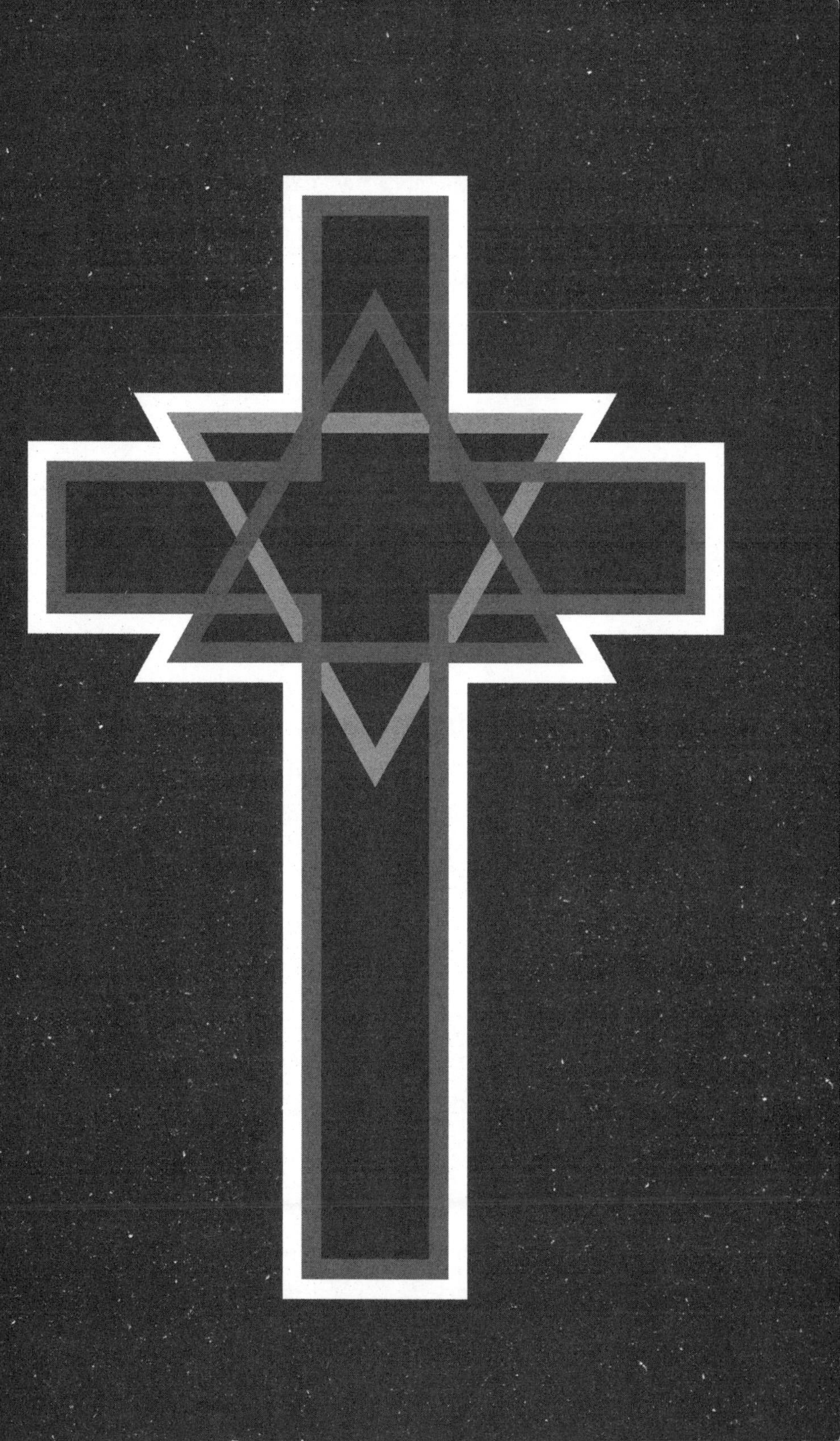

STUDY TITLE: "ON EARTH AS IT IS IN HEAVEN"

Old Covenant: Are celebrations important? Why?
Esther 9:27–28; 2 Chronicles 29:31; Deuteronomy 11:19

New Covenant: Who is our provider? Why do I have to rest?
John 6:1–14; Matthew 6:26–28

Poetry & Wisdom: What does God say that I must do to know him?
Psalm 46:10

† ✡ PRAYER ✡ †

Father, thank you for teaching us how to pray. Jesus, your words are life and glory and power. I pray like you said to pray, Lord, that your kingdom would come and your will would be done, on earth as it is in heaven. Let us know what heaven is like and let us live like that here. Thank you that there is no striving in your presence but there is the fullness of joy! And it's your joy that is our strength. You're our provider, so let us rest and be still so we can know you. Amen.

RANDOM ACTS OF KINDNESS AND TO-DO:

- ☐ Put on hour-long audio book, sermon, or worship set from YouTube and stretch 10 min., do kettlebell workout 20 min., run 20 min. with dog
- ☐ Worship with guitar
- ☐ Make roast, chicken soup, salmon, quinoa and roasted veggies, apple crumble, and sweet tea; buy challah; invite family and friends over for Shabbat!
- ☐ Clean out closet and make an office in there
- ☐ Give <u>The Barbarian Way</u> to Joelene

New Song Idea: "Life Screams"

Bm, A, G, Bm, F#, G · Chorus: G, D, A, B, A, G, A, B, G, A

Grand speeches pour out with the rain
On streets where no one's listening
You curse the cold wind on your face
> But she's trying to tell you something
A song unfolds in the distance, somehow you
 feel it in your soul
Somehow you carry on with your business like
 you didn't hear
This melody that calls you home

Life sings out, it's calling you by name
Life screams out that all of this will
 change
Your lungs are only flesh and
 everything that dies will fade away
Life calls for her lover, you will live
 forever

Sturm Shabbat Chicken Soup

1 whole chicken, 3-4 lbs. (Or use boneless, skinless chicken breast if you don't want to pull out bones. They're a tad less flavorful and tender but lots easier, in my opinion.)

4 qt. (4 32 oz. boxes) of chicken broth (or use the equivalent in Better Than Bouillon)

6 lg. carrots, sliced

6 celery stalks, including leaves, sliced

1 lg. sweet onion, whole

handful of fresh parsley, handful of fresh dill

2 tsp. black pepper, ½ tsp. cloves, salt to taste

cooked brown rice or quinoa

Cover chicken with broth in a large pot. Bring to boil. When foamy scum rises to top, pull pot off burner and skim it off. Add vegetables, herbs, and spices and bring to boil again. Then turn down heat and continue to simmer for at least 25 min. Chicken is done when its internal temperature is 165°F; carefully take the whole chicken from pot and put on a large sheet pan. Pull meat from the bones carefully. I use rubber gloves when I do this because it can be very hot. Discard the bones and skin and put meat back into pot. Continue to simmer up to two hours, if desired. Serve over rice or quinoa.

P.M. BIBLE READING

Old Covenant: Isaiah 58
New Covenant: Hebrews 4
Poetry & Wisdom: Psalm 62

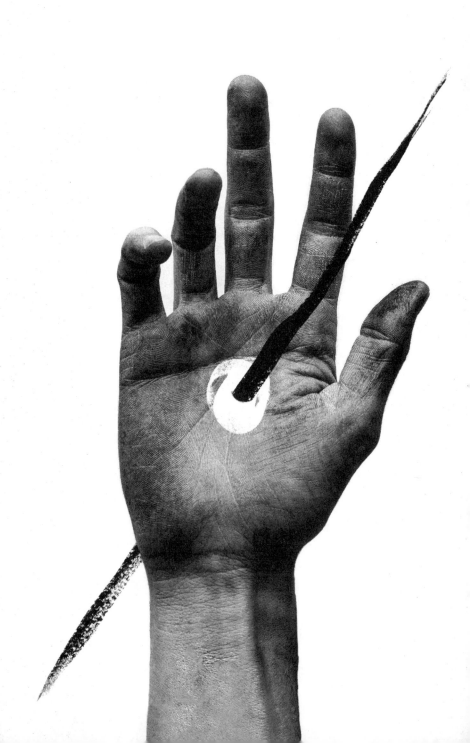

HEAVEN CULTURE

RETURNING MY REST

Reflection

Yesterday a new tradition started in our family: Purim and the movie *Trolls*.

The Wonder of Heaven on Earth

The Whosoevers are a group of my friends in the rock and extreme sports world who put on free events and tell their stories of overcoming addiction, gangs, abusive relationships, alcoholism, and suicide. We put on a rock show and talk about Jesus. Three Easters ago I traveled to Israel with the Whosoevers. Our tour guide, Yuval, was a Messianic Jew, a Jew who follows Christ.

Our trip to Jerusalem fell on a Sabbath. It's a powerful thing to see a whole city shut down. It begins with a dancing celebration with singing at the Western Wall at sunset on Friday to welcome in the "Shabbat."

God created the Sabbath to be a holy day of rest. A time when we remember how God made the earth and everything in it. Sabbath helps us further understand how God provides for us, physically and spiritually. God made everything we see with the words of his mouth because of his love and thoughtfulness and kindness—to remind us he is our Provider, our Protector, our good King, and our good Father. He didn't miss anything. Sabbath invites us to celebrate his goodness in a focused way.

Sabbath gives us eternal perspective. We realize that even though we work during the week, it is God who provides every gift we have on earth. Sabbath also reminds us of the treasure of family—family is our most precious gift. During our visit, we saw families gathered together, having picnics and reading the Scriptures to each other.

What a fascinating sight that was!

Many Christians think Sabbath is on Sunday. The Scriptures, however, tell us the Sabbath, or "Shabbat" as they call it in Israel, falls on Saturday, the seventh and last day of the week.

So why do we go to church on Sunday? The Scriptures call Sunday "the Lord's Day" because it was the day of the week Jesus rose from the dead. The reason we as Christians don't celebrate Shabbat on Saturday is not because Jesus moved Sabbath from Saturday to Sunday. It's because Jesus became our Sabbath.

The work of Jesus was connecting with God and loving people by teaching them, healing them, and blessing them. Jesus shows us what heaven-on-earth work looks like.

His work is Sabbath work.

His work is now our work.

We must work from a place of total peace and joy and trust. We must not work as if *our job* is providing for us or our money will save us.

We must work as though we are already citizens of heaven. We must view our work here on earth as if God himself assigned it to us. This perspective transforms our work into worship! We can worship him with joy because we get to do our work in his name here.

We live under Adam's curse when we *strive* and *sweat* for survival like the world around us that doesn't acknowledge God as a Father. But Jesus came to teach us how to be children of the kingdom—totally provided for. He even provided unique works for each of us to accomplish with our lives.[1]

And why do we work if we are in a perpetual Sabbath as Christians? Because we are called to bring God's kingdom to earth as it is in heaven. We do that everywhere we go, in everything we do.

We don't work as though we don't need faith. We have faith and therefore we work in response to our faith. Like the book of James says, "Without works our faith is dead" (see James 2:17).

But when we work, we work from the Sabbath of Christ. And we do it because of love. Our response to his love will be that we work. So we are always working and we are always resting.

Our good works may be a job at the mall. But we are still enjoying the Sabbath as long as in our hearts we have an open dialogue with God, making our work an intentional act of bringing the kingdom to earth as it is in heaven. Our Sabbath life should look like heaven on earth. That's what will mark our Sabbath.

Give It a Try

In Israel, our tour guide, Yuval, responded to our fascination with Shabbat. "Why don't you try to have a Shabbat on this day when you go home?" he said.

There is a Scripture I carry with reverence in the forefront of my mind whenever I hear someone give me advice like this: "Honor the prophet and receive the prophet's reward" (see Matt. 10:41).

1. Ephesians 2:10.

I thought, *The next time we're home long enough, I want to try.*
When we returned from Israel, we tried it. Those first three
Shabbats taught me so much. We observed Shabbat as a family, in
our own way. Each time was different. And what I started learning
was phenomenal.

First, I learned that I can get way too caught up in both housework and emails, news, texts, and social media. When I set my
heart to focus on my family and cultivate heaven in my home
among my family, I see heaven happen.

I see the love they feel. It's so tangible. To make such a feast
for them. To cease housework. To get off my phone. To make eye
contact for as long as they need it. To listen to their imaginations
and stories without interruption for as long as they want to share.
That's heaven! And it's here in my house!

I can run around the kitchen island with them as many times
as they want to until they get tired because I have nothing else to
do. I have nowhere else to be. I don't know what time it is, and it
doesn't matter.

I experience a sense of being timeless or eternal in these moments that I haven't found at any other time. There is no clock
for bedtime and no alarm for the morning. There is enough food
for everyone to eat for the next twenty-four hours. And there's no
work to be done, except the heavenly work of love and attention
given to the hearts of our family members.

My conversations with my husband on Shabbat become silly.
We talk more like friends. Our words are not about the business of
family and work and home that conversations can all degenerate
into during the week.

I saw, in the deep connections we made on these nights, how
the clock, my phone, and my chores can divide my heart up. I end
up giving my loved ones and the Lord even less of my heart than
when those things are not taking up the back of my mind.

The Shabbat atmosphere shines deeply with *heaven culture*.
It restores my heart.

And I believe it's also restorative to my family's hearts. It brings us back to the point of it all.

My husband has taken on the duties of cleaning up and doing dishes, and so do our guests at times. I think this is permissible because it is done as a "Thank you" and as an "I love you back" kind of gesture. It is not my husband's or my guests' ordinary work to do dishes or housework. It is an act of loving service. They bring heaven into my house with these gestures.

My love and appreciation for them puts me on the verge of tears because such beautiful gestures are not required or expected. On Shabbat I leave these duties undone on purpose because they are my ordinary work. I feel their worship of the Lord. The warmth of God's fire falling on their thankful sacrifice fills my home and my heart. It has blessed my relationships overwhelmingly.

Observing Shabbat shows me where I am lacking in the rest of the week and has changed the way I go about my time with my husband and children during the week. It's changed how I view the work in my home as well, making me aware when I step out of Shabbat in my heart.

The more I am reminded of a Sabbath heart position on Shabbat, the more I can "work" from that heart during the week. When I'm cleaning, answering emails, or looking at the clock and calendar, I can do it from a Sabbath heart and stay in dialogue with the Lord and open to my family.

I can remain in a place of rest and trust as the reordering of my priorities changes the landscape of my "plans" in a blessed way.

What time is it?

I heard a bell this morning. I thought about it in my asleep/awake cresting moment and considered a doorbell. I thought about the words of Christ in Revelation saying that he is at the door, knocking, and if we hear his voice and open the door that he will come in and dine with us. Maybe the bell was Jesus, ringing the doorbell of my heart, calling me to answer. Is there something I have to offer him to eat? What could I even think of to feed Jesus?

I could see Jesus knocking on the door, full of joy, holding all the wonders of the created universe and of love right in his smile. Right there behind his beautiful face, the breath of God that created me and the door he so graciously, gently, humbly "waits" behind. His skin filled with the oils of anointing that empower and heal and set right and provide and deliver. The anointing that breaks off every chain that would weigh us down, hold us back, or lead us in the wrong direction. Jesus, full of provision and wonder and wisdom, standing on the other side of the door, beaming and full of joy over his love for me.

When I invite him in, he doesn't say, "Here, Lacey, let me fix you. This is the question you are struggling with and here's the answer," or "Here is the money you need to provide for all your uncertainties." (Although he does and has said and done these things in various ways throughout my relationship with him.)

No, instead he says, "I've come to have dinner with you." I comply, breathless. I feel strange preparing food in front of him. I feel strange to continue my practice of talking to him in my mind as I rush about the kitchen. I'm so flustered at the honor of being given the opportunity to serve him that I can barely look at him. I ask him in my thoughts, as is my habit when I can't find something, *Oh, Lord, where is the honey?* The idea comes: *the cupboard,* and I glance up. His smile looks wider now, on the edge of laughter. I realize he can make honey pool up from the bottom of the cup if he likes. But I can see what he likes is the joy of letting me feel the rush of getting to serve him.

For a moment, I think of how the tea I'm making will taste, and then it hits me . . . the Scriptures, the Word of God, is sweeter than honey. I marvel, *How in the world can I improve the palate of Christ, the Word of God, sweeter than honey in the flesh?* With the thought comes this mixture of worshipful awe and a giving-up, verge-of-depression exasperation over the futility of offering Christ anything. The feeling crashes over me, and my throat tightens. My chest grows warm. I feel a rush like the swelling of thunder washing over me, and my eyes blur with tears.

"Thank you," he says out loud to me. His voice, his words go off like a bomb in my heart. I am trembling and sobbing violently on the inside. I have lost all strength, and my soul is lying prostrate on the floor of my inner being like a dead person. Worship and gratitude overtake me. I am somehow still outwardly finishing the preparation for his tea. My eyes pour with tears, but this is the only outward sign of my inner throne room experience. I place the cup before him and realize that all my days, from the moment I met him at sixteen, I have only ever longed with everything in me to live for him and please him. His words are still thundering in my soul. I feel his pleasure over me. I wrestle with the absurdity of the One who deserves all glory and honor and praise saying thank you to the one he made and rescued.

I sit and finally look into his face again. Jesus is beaming with joy. He lifts the tea to his mouth without taking his smiling gaze from mine. I can see he knows the taste, temperature, and everything there is to know about the tea before he drinks at all. He knows every bee and flower that participated in the honey-making, the beekeeper, and the harvesters; the cow that made the cream, the farmer, and

his family; the ones who grew the tea leaves, dried them, and packaged them; the company who made the cup he is sipping from, the one who started the company, and their family; the truck driver who brought it to the store; the loaders who put it in the warehouse, the boxers and stockers who put it on the shelf . . . the cashier who checked me out when I bought it . . . where every dollar that paid for it came from . . . every hand the money flowed through since it was deemed a credit. All of this knowledge and so much more pushes sheer joy through his smile as he goes to drink. He closes his eyes as he takes it in, delighted at the contact. I marvel, eyes still pouring tears.

"Well done!" He laughs as he lowers the cup. I know he has said this to all of us, even the bees. I can feel the blessing of his words spread like gamma rays through me, going out to each creature connected to it . . . even the fields where tea leaves continue growing. His breath becomes a wind that makes the whole field tremble. His blessing ripples and I want to fall into a heap on the floor, but for some reason I stay seated just fine.

Now we are sitting silently. He looks at me with joy and love and peace. All of this fills the room, and we just sit. All of a sudden I understand something I have not understood before. My Lord just wants to be my friend. Not my teacher, not my overseer, not my provider, not my corrector. He doesn't want repentance from me or even traditional worship in this moment. This desire of his is what is giving me the grace to just sit with him instead of fall on the floor. He didn't come to be served but he humored me. His mouth already tasted like honey, but still he enjoyed my tea.

Then I thought of my friend Jasmine, how, at a time when I had stopped believing in friendship, she had ministered friendship to me just this way. Nothing to do. No business to attend to. No teaching me or wanting me to teach her. No obligation to me as family, no wanting me to meet any needs for her. No trying to meet any needs

for me. She just came to sit quietly with me. Maybe watch movies. Maybe just drink tea. After six months of her ministry, I realized she was just a friend. A true friend. Not a "what can I get from you and what can you get from me" friend. Just a "let's hang out and just be together" friend. I see that this is what Christ wanted this morning when I heard the bell ring.

Hello, Lord. Would you like some tea?

Everyday Heaven

Weight in my soul
Light in your eyes
Wake me up and show me life
Hold back tears
Lay down rights
Give up years to eternal life
Worth it all
Worth the fight
Writing Truth on my soul tonight
Lies are loud
Truth will stand
Freedom lives in every man
Fighting a battle that's already won
Lay down arms
Rival the sun
Burning bright in future past
Play for the Father
Make him laugh
Inside I rest with present eyes
Watch life unfold
The great surprise
Love never ends
So don't stop exploring
Hope isn't passive
Heaven isn't boring

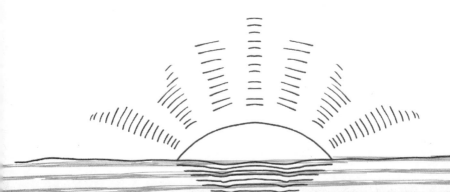

Study Title: "Learning from God in Your Circumstances and God in Others"

Old Covenant: What does the Lord require of people?
Micah 6:8

New Covenant: Why are other perspectives important?
Hebrews 5:8–9; Matthew 7:5; Ephesians 5:21

Poetry & Wisdom:
Proverbs 27:17

PRAYER

Father, thank you for another day. Thank you for all the ways you've shaped me and all the ways you've let me shape the world around me. I ask for grace to cover my space and grace to fulfill your purpose. Let me be humbler and always listen to how you're speaking through other people who have a different perspective than I do. Help me to hang on to the pearls of wisdom that you've given me and help me to be careful not to let them be stolen or trampled by others who don't understand what you've taken me through. I love you, Daddy. Amen.

RAK & To-Do:

- run 20 min. with dog, do kettlebells
- Make fruit salad for family game night
- Clean out the bus for tour
- Work on book
- Read Ender's Game

New Song Idea: "Seed Sown in Tears"

Verse: Am, F, C, B · Chorus: Am, F, C, G

Verse: I'm the one holding you in suffering
And I am with you in the sorrow.
I'll be your strength when you're struggling
And turn today into tomorrow.
There's more to overcome
More light to shine, more love.
There's hope for you to bring
So stand up in the pain and sing.

Chorus: You are my song, my poetry
Beloved, precious humanity . . .

····[RECIPE:]····
Sturm Family Favorite Fruit Salad

SAUCE:
juice of one lemon
    or ¼ cup
juice of two oranges
    or ½ cup
¼ cup honey
¼ tsp. ground cloves
¼ tsp. vanilla

FRUIT:
1 chopped apple, 1 chopped pear
2 cups chopped strawberries
1 cup blueberries
1 cup pineapple chunks
5 mandarin oranges, sections sliced
    into halves
2 bananas, sliced

Combine all sauce ingredients and bring
to a boil, then simmer 5 min. Remove
from heat and let cool. Mix all fruit
together, pour cooled sauce over salad,
toss gently, cover, and put in the fridge.
Serve chilled.

PM THROUGH THE BIBLE READING:

Old Covenant: Isaiah 60
New Covenant: Revelation 21
Poetry & Wisdom: Psalm 27

this/short/reminder/of/d

is/to/remind/one/that/life/in/itse

a/blinking/of/an

Memento Mori

this/short/reminder/of/death/
remind/one/that/life/itself/is
a/blinking/of/an/eye

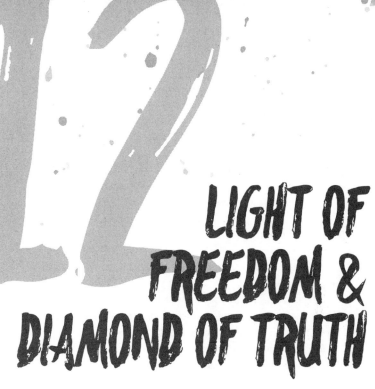

LIGHT OF FREEDOM & DIAMOND OF TRUTH

RETURNING MY FREEDOM

Reflection

My head was spun around over and over in an effort to humble
myself
    (I was indeed humbled by the Lord first)
    having been deceived.
    Having broken my own words and expectations of myself in that
what I did not think I was capable of doing
    (because of disgust of sin)
    I ended up doing with zealousness and blinded eyes, considering
my actions superiorly moral—and
    (to all my opposition of course)
    righteous in my deception.

When I found that my self-righteous rebellion was truly rebellion against God, I looked up and realized I had run far out from underneath God's protective covering.

(How could anyone expect God to bless, protect, or take good care of them when they refuse to heed any of the warnings he gave for protection? Like the warning against committing adultery? Adultery, which is a sin like all others, that he warned leads to death?)

I had chosen, in my deception, to build a platform.

Over and over—quietly, with demonic protection, I chose sin. And that sin built a platform for the enemy of my soul to operate from in my life.

I gave him a stage to work from—a high building towering above everything in my life.

Satan simply took my sin and quietly stepped up, sin by sin, higher and higher, until the day it came for him to reveal his intentions for me. I was now blinded by a thick darkness clouding my whole mind and soul. On this day, the lion-sized enemy of suicide that God had rebuked at my salvation was now a screeching, horrifying, dinosaur-sized monster, circling above me, and I was doomed.

Becoming Humble through Making Bad Choices

In this place of darkness, I fell, weak and empty and crushed in my soul. I was lying on my face, ready to die in my utter worthlessness, when a warrior poet came by my room with a story that breathed on my dead heart, revealing that within me lay a faint, dying ember of faith. Perhaps I could stay alive past my shame, past my false sense of being a god for people I couldn't save, past being a liar to myself, past my worthlessness and hopelessness. One ember that might turn at a simple story filled with illuminating words.

I came awake trembling, empty, poor, and humble.

In my openness, I turned this way and that way, fell into ditch after ditch, with a willingness to change and be wrong in every direction. I found so many things that were wrong in my judgments.

My friend Melanie said, "Lacey, don't lose yourself."

But what she didn't understand was that I had lost myself when I blinded my own eyes in sin. I lost myself when the fires of my choices blazed through my life, revealing what was worth anything at all for what it was, and burning up what wasn't eternal or worth anything. I existed in the charred remains of a city built on many lies I'd believed. I had nothing to judge anymore.

I sat knowing nothing.

I knew nothing of myself except humiliation.

I knew nothing of God except to tremble at his undeserved mercy.

I knew his wisdom was unfathomable.

I knew the size of God, compared to my own little self, was unknowable.

I knew nothing of life, except that I had, in God's unsearchable love, been given another chance to live here on earth, before he takes my life back.

So in my total surrender, I became as open, innocent, wondering, limp, and weak as an infant or a leaf in the wind. I was rendered utterly poor in spirit to wonder in awe at the truth—which turned out to be so much more than the line in the sand I had tried to turn it into so often.

Truth is more like a multifaceted diamond that is absolutely solid, infinitely multifaceted in the colors and light it produces. And it's important to be humble in the face of truth being revealed. As the diamond turns, the revelation we receive changes from one color to the next.

But what we understand isn't changing from one shifting sand mound to another. It is unfolding, as we perceive the multifaceted light pouring out into our lives, at different times and in different ways, coming from the unshakable, unbreakable, solid, and unchangeable source that is the diamond of truth.

Jesus said, "I am the way and the truth and the life" (John 14:6).

He is living, speaking, and freeing at all times, saying in so many situations, *There is no right or wrong, only your choice to respond in the freedom of your will. So choose, and let others choose, and make no room for condemnation; for God alone will judge the thoughts and intentions of his servants. You are not God, little, tiny steward.*

So I began, in my openness and innocence, emptiness and humility, to consider, to be wide-eyed and teachable, learning without judgment in every place I came to.

One of the judgments that fell away was one I had been raised with against middle-class and wealthy white people. Their ways were so foreign to my understanding and experience. I felt oppressed by them, misunderstood, unseen, condemned, and untouchable to them for most of my life. I judged them as selfish and greedy. I judged them as belittling and condemning.

I judged them as ignorant and judgmental. From my short, small interactions with a few of them, I had made an overarching condemnation of all people who looked this way to me.

But as I grew in relationship with the God who made all people, loves all people, and has them all in his hands, I began to see more from his perspective. Once I realized that the pride I judged in them was rooted in my own pride, I realized I was wrong, and my heart was softened.

I hated so much their blind obedience to rules. They seemed to me to be willingly ignorant and foolish, making life harder on the poor because of a rule that had no face or difficult consequence they could feel behind it.

But once I realized that rebellion was stealing so many things from my life (like a deeper faith and trust, and at times the ability to tell right from wrong, which had almost succeeded in stealing my life through suicide), I softened to the point of wanting to learn more about what they knew.

The greed I had witnessed and despised in them seemed stingy and materialistic in the face of so many hungry and poor people around them. So their greed was countered by my foolish giving, where I would break my word financially in one place so I could pretend to be a financial savior in another, trying to save someone who didn't want to be saved. I would try to hold a door open financially for someone when God was closing it, and I would end up getting slammed in it. While condemning their greed, I was pouring the resources God had given me into pockets with holes in them. It wasn't until God rebuked me for bad stewardship that I was softened toward these people and their ways with resources.

I saw them as selfish and disgusting because of that. I couldn't understand how they could go on vacations when people needed so much around them, or how they could have a big house and not invite the poor to live with them.

How could they be so unmoved by the heartbreaking situations around them and carry on with family dinner?

Meanwhile, I was letting people control, manipulate, emotionally blackmail, use, and abuse me to the point that I was physically falling apart and not able to fulfill what I knew for certain God had called me to do. I watched all of the peace and joy that God had given me stolen because I would not honor my freedom to say no.

Then I began to respect the way I saw them protect their own personal peace in their circles, and I saw their genuine joy because of boundaries they had placed around their decisions and hearts and respect for the choices and boundaries of others. So I began to consider this group of people I had condemned with a new openness.

From this new place of consideration, I learned about choosing and following peace, about self-preservation—which in the midst of self-destruction is revolutionary and life-giving.

I learned about saying things in the right way at the right time. Before I just screamed whatever I was thinking in the name of being honest and real. Which, most of the time, just hurt people and made them not listen or hear anymore.

I learned about considering results and weighing reactions. I learned about meeting people where they were and not demanding they meet me where I was or else writing them off completely. My ways were no better. I grew up thinking that if you have a problem with someone you say it to their face, and if you talk behind someone's back you are worse than their enemy. But I realize now that, in their eyes, venting to someone else instead of speaking to someone's face can also be a self-reflective processing act taken in order to be kind, keep peace, and then genuinely forgive, forget what happened, and move on.

But, of course, that can become a breeding ground for gossip and backbiting. Just like speaking your grievances to someone's face can become a breeding ground for emotional or verbal abuse, false accusations, and cursing. I found this difference to be the most revolting in them, and they found it most revolting and uncivilized in me.

I found comfort in the fighting, even if it was abusive, for it felt honest.

The cold peace, even if repressive or disingenuous, was what they found comfort in, for it felt kind and ordered and merciful.

Prejudice

One day I was forced to consider the differences and also consider that I might be wrong, in order to humble myself. This was because I think God wanted me to confront and abolish my prejudice. I had invited God to be as much a part of picking the person whom I would marry as I was. I wrote about this miraculous journey in my second book, *The Mystery*.

But, as I share in that book, it was clear that God led me to Joshua Sturm. I married a man from a family that was, outwardly, so much of what I had grown up feeling alienated from. It wasn't until I lived in this amazing family and became part of a similar community that I even began to realize I was prejudiced against this kind of way of life.

The differences popped up everywhere.

In my journey to humble myself, I let go of my prejudices and, in many ways, adopted their way of doing life. In my mind, I was doing it in faith, considering, perhaps, there was something better for me and what God had called me to do in their way of living and thinking. In many ways, it was a complete 180 from how I was naturally inclined to operate.

So I have struggled through to navigate my heart, to see what God is saying through my new family and community, and to celebrate it with humility when I don't understand it all fully.

Last night I was watching a film in which different people read Martin Luther King Jr.'s *Letter from a Birmingham Jail*. I felt, after all these years of having no judgments, that my whole heart was being stirred up again.

I was like a pot filled with different layers—carrots and onions on the bottom, then the celery, then potatoes, then broth and meat on top. It was as if, in each new season of my life, I had to leave behind something I learned in order to grab on to the next lesson that seemed to contradict it.

I had left the onions and carrots and veggies and was sitting up here on top of the meat, feeling slightly disoriented but determined to stay focused on what I was called to see right in front of me. Holding on to the latest truth I had found and forgetting all that had come before it. But here, through this film about Martin Luther King Jr., God used his words like a big spoon to stir the pot—and all the flavors were being mixed together.

I had experienced only one flavor and fragrance at a time, but as I watched, I began to smell something totally new. Instead of smelling only the scent at the top of the pot, now I could smell all the flavors blending together into a new, tantalizing, signature, beckoning song.

What is that?! my heart began to rumble and wonder. *I've never smelled such a glorious fragrance*, my soul mused.

I realize now that, in my desire to understand and to stay humble and open, I had done what my friend Melanie warned me against.

I had lost part of myself. Indeed, I needed to die and forget everything in order to heal properly.

But, as it turns out, it is not God's will that I become a stereotypical middle-class or wealthy white person. And I am *not* to condemn them.

I am to be influenced by their fragrance.

I am to change my own flavor a bit.

But I am to remain myself.

I am to honor all that I have encountered and to learn and grow and change according to the way the Lord is moving my heart, in all the ways that he does that.

I am responsible to steward my encounters, but stewardship feels most times like a hands-off, "I trust you" kind of stance from God. So many of our differences are permissible differences. We are a multifaceted gem, displaying the wisdom of God in our differences while united in our core, which is the gospel of Jesus Christ.

Whether it's my family I married into, the community I live in, the churches I visit and minister to, or the organizations I work with, they are meant to change me and I am meant to change them. God has always intended that we learn from each other. And in a desire to take the lowest seat and learn on my end, I have neglected in many cases to value my own part that I am meant to bring to the table. I have questioned myself and laid down and tried to change when I should have been kindly and lovingly and peacefully inviting change on their side as well.

As I watched and listened to the words of Martin Luther King Jr., he spoke of the "moderate white." I realized that much of my being placed in this culture as an adult was God's intention for me and for the ones around me.

Martin Luther King Jr. talked of his disappointment with the moderate white church, and in his balanced wisdom he held honor and respect for his brothers and sisters while still acknowledging his own function to sharpen them and keep himself sharp. His definitions of law and authority and justice were so powerful and helped pull me out of the ditches of both passive, complacent slavery and total rebellion.

Indeed, the road of the righteous is narrow but leaves room for the Father to speak on all matters, in all moments blurring lines at will and drawing them again, all according to the very solid, unmovable Diamond of Truth that Christ is.

Every shift and change I have encountered has been established through tears, writing, teaching, and sharing. And this shift in me is monumental and is no different.

Yes, I was wrong about foolishly giving what God didn't tell me to give, but we are wise about the importance of generosity. So may I bring that with me into the flavor of generosity and let it influence the smart budgeters, the investors and businesspeople.

Yes, I was wrong about saying whatever I think whenever I like, but we are wise about honesty and being genuine. So may I bring the flavor of honesty and a genuine heart into the peacekeeping quiet of those who don't like loud voices.

Yes, I was wrong about not having any boundaries and letting myself be taken advantage of, and unknowingly trying to cross others' boundaries, but we are wise about being compassionate, recognizing our neediness at times, and having a loving, joyful willingness to suffer and sacrifice for others. So I will bring the flavor of compassion and sacrifice into those who are wise about knowing where they begin and I end, knowing the sovereignty of God, knowing what they are called to and what they are not, and knowing how to follow peace.

May I always honor my own freedom and honor the freedom of others.

May our freedom be the fiercely protected gift from God that his church esteems above all else.

May this be our chief aim in our unity as believers, because freedom is light that shines on the diamond of truth, and love is the rainbow of colors that shoot out from every direction.

There is no rainbow of love displayed without the light of freedom. You must have freedom to have love. So let us honor freedom in every way we can.

May we each recognize which flavors to change and which ones to be changed by. May we all be one glorious, fragrant bowl of worship to the Father. May the Lord delight in and feast on the marinated, colorful combination of flavors we willingly, joyfully, and lovingly bring to his table.

I had a picture in my mind of people who didn't take offense but genuinely considered without offense what others were saying, no matter the style or delivery.

I saw people just freely thinking, freely speaking, and freely responding, with no secret thinking of offensive things or accusations about the other person.

I saw totally secure people who knew they were loved, who didn't need approval of others; people who weren't sensitive to take offense and who never blamed someone else for "making them feel" a certain way.

I saw people who took responsibility and charge over their own hearts and emotions and dealt with them before God, humbly before others.

I saw absolute freedom and true love and true intimacy. And the ability to be true selves.

Is it right to tiptoe around someone's unrighteous offense triggers? For you it may be an act of seeking peace, but it's as Martin Luther King Jr. described: a cold peace, not a true peace.

Indeed, for you it may be intended to be an act of true humility, but it also may very well be a self-imposed act of enslaving yourself in subtle ways.

Any act of self-imposed slavery in your heart or mind is a chain to the demonic. We operate in the demonic when we violate our own will to please someone else. This isn't to be confused with laying down our wants and desires willingly to love someone; that is the mark of the truest kind of love. Slavery is violating the will. Being manipulated, blackmailed, controlled, and forced under threat of punishment.

To do what someone else wants above what we want may be an act of love, but when it is love, we are joyful, peaceful, and generous, and there is a loving desire to lay down what we want for the other person. The loving desire is more free and dominant than our own preference.

This is not slavery; this is freedom used in love. It is righteous. But to "willingly" do what someone else wants when it violates the use of our free will, that is us putting chains on ourselves.

I hate hot pink. But my husband loves it on me. I wear hot pink shoes because I love my husband and the shoes remind us of our differences and how much I love that we are different.

Now, if I hate hot pink shoes and I wear them with a grudge or a sense of martyrdom, like, *Well, I don't get to pick; I just have to do this because he likes it*, then I have put myself in chains. He can't "make me feel" any kind of way. I choose to violate my own will under the "excuse" of feeling controlled or manipulated. But he can't control or manipulate me without me choosing to allow it, and in the end it is my wrong, not his.

If he were to throw all my shoes away except for the hot pink ones and take all my money away so I couldn't buy any new ones, then my reason for wearing hot pink shoes that I don't want to would be different. I would have no choices.

But I choose whether or not to put them on my feet, to keep them on my feet, to object, or to express that I do not like them. It's when I blame my husband for making me feel or do something I don't want that I must step back and see if I am honoring my own free will or if I am violating it.

If we honored everyone's freedom and our own freedom, then no one would take offense or falsely blame others for their feelings or actions. And we could be free to express ourselves and accept and honor each other's choices and perspectives and preferences.

And offense would be difficult.

Prophetic Joy and Sorrow

If I could see the way you stood beside me for fifty
   years,
The way we grew together, sorrow laughter tears
If I could see you stand up in your purpose seizing time
Assured that nothing ever stolen was ever yours
   or mine
Flipping all around for glory, testifying with faith
I could champion you every moment of every single day
I could love you in a way that gently passes through the
   storms
Knowing love endures forever while heaven's glory comes
Lord, let me see those things, have mercy let me see
You said blessed are those who don't see and yet still
   believe.
If this is a better way, I will write it on my wrist
So long as I don't waste these moments of uncertainty
   with fits
Worry distance seeing weeds, don't let that be the way
   I wait
If all it takes for me to love with gracious hope and
   faith
Is to see a glimpse of the futures and then hope for the
   most glory.
Then let me have the glimpse for peace, and I'll ever
   share the story.
I want a glimpse but I want you most. I want to touch
   your heart.
I'm choosing the forever life and forever is where I'll
   start.

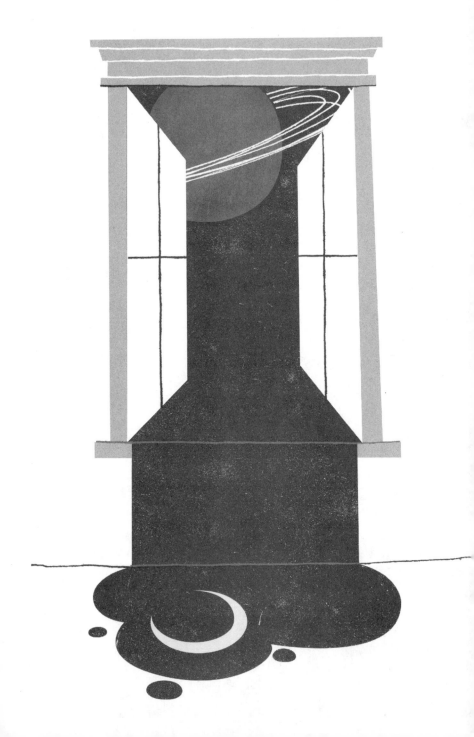

POSTLUDE

HEAVEN ON EARTH

Preaching to Trees

Walking through the woods this morning, preaching to the trees, I concluded: if your task doesn't lead to love, then you have not accomplished the purpose of the task.

I die today.

I face God.

I recognize my whole life was a test.

Life is not a test like in school that is all about whether or not I will pass or fail.

What is my time on earth a test of?

This life is a test of the will.

The human will is absolutely free, and the will shapes the soul. It is like the spinal cord of the soul. It is with the will that I hold on and let go of what's in my soul. It is with the will that we bind life to and loose death from our souls.

We have different portals into the soul. Our eyes and ears are a couple of the ways we let in ideas, images—spiritual life or death. When we speak, we will have either life or death on our tongues.

Our speech attempts to make a sort of contract with our souls, and if a person is willing (with their freedom) to receive what we say, our speech will attempt to make a contract with their soul as well.

When others violate us, and we feel controlled or coerced and start to point our fingers and blame the world, we cannot forget our free will. In these moments, our very own free will stands as the most important possession in life.

Are we willing, or not?

This will be where the eyes of God are. Right in our souls, looking for courage in us to stand up in our freedom, to honor our freedom the best we are able.

The question in every moment is never What are they *making me* feel/do/think? but rather Okay, they did this; now what am I going to do/say/think? What will I choose with my freedom? How will I respond with my free will?

God has loved us and encouraged us to love. Will we love? God trusts us.

When God gave Adam the choice between life and death, it was in this moment that God created love with freedom, for humanity.

He loved Adam by trusting him with freedom to choose.

God doesn't explain his actions to us, because even in his non-explanation, he is giving us the freedom to choose to judge him or trust in him.

Even when he approves of Abel's sacrifice over Cain's, he doesn't defend himself. He just lets us read and honors the freedom of every reader to choose to condemn God as harsh and wrong out of suspicion and accusation or to choose to trust God as just, beyond what we can know, out of love for him.

When Cain was tempted with bitterness and anger, God, in his love, warned Cain about sin.

"Sin is crouching at your door. It desires to have you, but you must master it" (see Gen. 4:6–8).

Even when God could see that Cain's choice to remain bitter and angry would lead to the destruction of his own soul, by turning him into the world's first murderer, and the destruction of Abel's physical body and his physical impact on the earth, by becoming a victim of his brother's choice to grow in bitterness, God didn't stop it. He only warned.

Why? Because human freedom is that important to God. He honors the authority he gave us to rule with on the earth.

Freedom is eternally tied to love.

This life is filled with limited time, and daily choices are all about testing our will and God loving us through honoring our freedom.

God considers freedom worth dying for.

Abel was the first to physically die at the cost of freedom.

God honored Cain's freedom to choose the sin of murder.

There was no human to stand up for Abel and protect him in that moment. But if I had been there, witnessing the scene would have been a test of my will. Would I say something or do something to stop the murder if I could? Do I agree that Cain is right in his actions? Do I care only for myself? Would I be willing to lay down my life in an attempt to save others? This becomes a test of my likeness to God.

If we do not stand up as humans to defend the freedom and right to life that belongs to our human brothers and sisters, then we are not choosing to be like the God who created us. We are not honoring him as our Father.

We must do what we can to keep the innocent from being killed. We don't do this in order to control Cain but to honor and protect Abel's freedom and right to life.

If we don't honor Abel's freedom to live by protecting his life from Cain however we can, then we are not honoring freedom at all. We are not honoring God, who gave us freedom.

When we begin to disrespect and dishonor the freedom of others through complacency, laziness, selfishness, fear, control, fighting, violence, anger, murder, and other evils, then we have forfeited our own right to freedom by violating others'.

Cain was free to murder Abel only because no one intervened to rescue him.

God will honor our freedom to the death.

Abel's innocence and trust of his brother were beautiful and righteous.

Cain continued to choose bitterness, anger, and a callousness toward God in order to follow through with his sin of murder. But a witness must honor and protect Abel from violations of his freedom and right to life at all costs.

Sometimes this may mean that Cain's life is cut short too so that he will not continue in bitter or angry murdering of people. But perhaps there is a time for him to be given a chance to be sorry and turn his heart around. The kindness of forgiveness may woo him with godlike, merciful love and turn him completely from murdering and bitterness toward humility and honoring all life.

This is a new level of freedom that we have in Christ. The freedom he gives us of more time means extra chances to make choices to reject death, embrace Christ's forgiveness through his crucifixion and resurrection, and choose life.

This humble admission of guilt and humble crying out for a fresh start produce a free-loving, teachable heart that brings life instead of death and honors God.

This is when we begin to live the way we were created to.

This is when we begin to live like God's children on the earth.

When we die physically, we *return* to our maker. We face him and answer for what we have done with our lives. He has loved us by giving us the gift of life.

Life has screamed out his love for us all along. He has trusted us and invested in us life, earth, relationships, children, animals, natural talents, spiritual gifts, resources, money, time, a body, his written Scripture, his Son's blood for the forgiveness of our sin, his Holy Spirit to empower us to overcome, trials, pain, opportunities to have our faith strengthened, and moments to suffer for truth and righteousness and love.

Will he find that we have learned love when we meet him as the soul that outlasts the body? What *return* will he gain on his investment in us?

Will he have our hearts, our love, our faith, our trust, our lives poured out, our will yielded to his?

Are you my child?

God questions so we will reflect on the answers that he already knows.

God's Questions to Me

Do you look like me?

Have you learned love?

What did you do with the freedom you were given? I gave man freedom in the Garden. A wrong choice in a righteous place. A death choice in a place of life. A poor choice in a rich place.

Why did I give you this choice to make? Because I trusted you and had faith in you. This is what comes when I love.

I gave you the choice because I love you and gave you freedom. Giving you choice created freedom for you. I gave you responsibility over my tender and precious and rich creation.

I trusted you with it. I gave you life on earth and time to choose and redemption from death through the sacrifice of my Son, King Jesus Christ the Messiah.

I gave you his example of how to live fully the way you were created to. I gave you his Word written down and spoken to you, a love letter for you to seek and find me through.

I gave you my Spirit to empower you when you put your hope in Christ. I gave you my Holy Spirit so you could understand my personality and my loving motivations, and you could gain heavenly wisdom rooted in my holiness.

My Holy Spirit was sent to you by my Son Jesus Christ, the Prince of Peace.

So what did you do with the gift of Jesus? I gave you my love.

What did you do with my love?

Are you my child?

Do you look like me?

Have you learned love?

My Response to God

I thought about this as I walked through the woods early in the morning. It struck me how God will not ask if we got the laundry done, how many books or blogs we've written, how many songs we know or sang, if we ate healthy, or if we made people happy.

These are questions people around us ask that make us feel guilty and enslave us to their opinions of right and wrong. No. God won't ask about our earthly achievements that are important in the world's eyes.

He will ask about our souls' growth that is measured by his gaze where no one else sees, in moments the world may even scoff at or ridicule as a waste of time or irresponsible. He will ask if we learned to love.

We can feel his gaze on our souls like a hot laser burning and glowing on situations that are filled with his love. This is what we chase after. We will feel his grief when we have run ahead of love for the sake of a task or religion, or stayed behind love for the sake of politics, or blamed others for the sake of slavery.

In these moments of feeling his grief or the cold shiver that comes to our souls when his warmth is so obviously lifted, we must turn. Whatever it takes to run to him, we must run to him. Sometimes that means lying on our faces, praying in tongues, walking through the woods, going somewhere to be alone, fasting from soul clutter and distractions—forcing ourselves to remember that we must stop and turn!

Whatever it takes to stop the grief of his Holy Spirit. Whatever you do, don't numb yourself, close your eyes, or plug your ears to his grief over your thoughts or actions. Be brave and face him; listen and turn.

Whatever you do, don't get used to his sadness or his absence. Whatever you must do, stay hungry for the presence of God. Don't fill up on garbage that makes you feel empty and stuffed at the same time when you're done. Whatever you do, stay hungry.

How do we start?

With a conversation with God.

Prayer

God? Help.

I know I will face you one day. I don't want to waste time or opportunities.

Help, God.

Show me how to stop and follow you. You are where life begins and ends here and turns into life eternal. God, I want to be made right with you so I can come close. Draw me in and whisper your truth to my heart.

And when you do, let me not doubt you or talk myself out of or let myself be talked out of believing in you. Protect me from deceiving myself into choosing death. Show me where I have chosen death and deliver me from all of these choices.

I choose by an act of my will to loose from my soul all darkness. If I have given any part of my soul to any person, place, or thing, I call it back to me now. Come back, bits of my soul, so you can be whole! And I loose from my soul any part of any person, place, or thing that doesn't bring life and shouldn't be there.

I desire to let my life bring you glory and to become all that you created and intended me to be. I choose you, God. Thank you for the blood of Jesus that blots out my choices for death, in eternity.

Thank you for forgiving me of my sins by this great price you paid with your blood. Holy Spirit of God Almighty and Jesus Christ, I invite you to come and live in my soul.

Write the Word of God on my heart so that I won't sin against you. Holy Spirit, empower me to overcome every temptation that would lead to death. I invite you to show me truth whenever I am believing a lie. I invite you to fill me every day with your ideas and your love and your hope and your joy.

I pray you would remind me to cry out to you when I am getting lost and don't know what to do. I invite you, Father, to love me and discipline me in your love so that I will be protected from running into death. Please intervene so that I don't deceive myself. Thank you for your love. Thank you for your forgiveness. Strengthen me with the power of your Holy Spirit, who raised Christ from the dead.

So give me new life and let me do the works that you planned in advance for me to do, and as Jesus said, Lord, let me do the greater works he spoke of. Not ever out of performance, pride, or a lust for power but rather out of love, faith, humility, and glory that will go to you alone, as King of kings and Lord of lords.

I declare that you are Lord of my life. Give me discernment to know your voice and to love your Scriptures and your presence more than anything in the world. Let me know the difference between my voice, your voice, and the voice of the enemy who can disguise himself as an angel of light.

Protect me from deception and give me strong discernment.

Remove condemnation and judgment from my heart so that I won't be condemned.

Let me know you alone, hear your voice, accept what you say, and do what you say out of love. Bring people into my life who love you. Bring people who will confirm what you want to say to me with your Scriptures and with the security that comes from following your ways, which all lead to peace.

Give me wisdom from heaven.

Give me eyes to see, ears to hear, and a heart to understand.

Give me your thoughts and show me clearly how to hear your voice like daily bread.

Speak, Lord, your servant is listening.

A Lacey-Journal-Reader-Help

After you have prayed this, God is with you.

God is in you.

Don't take the reality and magnitude of this for granted. Having a relationship with God is the most important thing in life. Don't neglect it. Treat it the way you would any relationship.

Talk to God. And listen for him to speak to you. Write down any question you want to ask God, like this:

God, what do you want to say to me?

God, what do you think about me?

God, what do you want me to know about you?

Now write down anything you feel like God is saying.

Find three people who love the Scriptures and love you with no ulterior motives. Ask them what they think about what you have written.

If you hear something that goes against Scripture, just adjust your thoughts to the Scriptures and keep pressing in and asking him more questions. I believe that when we seek with all our hearts we will find him.

Truth is always speaking.

Let's tune in to that truth through the Scriptures, quieting our hearts, listening, and paying attention to how he is answering.

The truth we find in the Word of God and knowing his voice will bring us freedom.

It will pave the way for heaven to return to earth, as Jesus taught us to pray: "Your kingdom come, your will be done, on earth as it is in heaven" (Matt. 6:10).

So let us return to our Creator in our hearts. Let us live in a way that helps return heaven to earth.

illustrated
reflections by:
Josh Sturm

written reflections
by: Lacey Sturm

Lacey Sturm is a mother, wife, writer, speaker, and musician. Originally the voice behind the platinum-selling international rock band Flyleaf, she released her first solo project in 2016, which debuted at #1 on the Billboard Hard Rock Album chart. Lacey knows she is one of God's works of art, and she wants others to know and understand how special, how beautiful, how kaleidoscopically wonderful we are all made. Lacey speaks and performs in many diverse venues ranging from mainstream rock festivals to conferences to churches. She has been involved for many years with the Billy Graham Evangelistic Association, The Whosoevers, and Pulse. She lives in Pennsylvania with her family. For more information, visit www.laceysturm.com.

TRUE LOVE *exists*—
and it's worth pursuing.

Through raw, honest, and personal stories, Lacey Sturm shows you why true love is difficult and often painful—but still worth it. On the journey she recognizes destructive patterns in her own relationships, heals from past wounds, finds a way to trust again, and discovers a vision for a flourishing love that heals us, frees us—and is something we can believe in.

ALSO BY

LACEY STURM

Once a suicidal atheist, now a Christ-following rock artist,
Lacey tells her story of finding purpose behind the pain,
sharing the many reasons for her hope and helping readers
see how valuable they are to God.

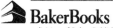

CONNECT WITH LACEY

and see her upcoming events at

LACEYSTURM.COM

@LaceySturm   @OfficialLaceySturm   LaceySturm81   LaceySturm81

LIKE THIS
BOOK?
Consider sharing it with others!

- Share or mention the book on your social media platforms. Use the hashtag **#TheReturnBook**.

- Write a book review on your blog or on a retailer site.

- Pick up a copy for friends, family, or anyone who you think would enjoy and be challenged by its message.

- Share this message on **FACEBOOK**: **"I loved #TheReturnBook by @LaceySturm81"**

- Share this message on **TWITTER**: **"I loved #TheReturnBook by @LaceySturm"**

- Share this message on **INSTAGRAM**: **"I loved #TheReturnBook by @OfficialLaceySturm"**

- Recommend this book for your church, workplace, book club, or class.

- Follow Baker Books on social media and tell us what you like.

   f **Facebook.com/ReadBakerBooks**

   y **@ReadBakerBooks**